advan

"Katherine Malmo has written an unflinching, unsentimental, profoundly moving, wickedly funny (*yes, I said funny*) deeply courageous book detailing one woman's diagnosis, treatment and recovery from inflammatory breast cancer. These stories are made of a fictioneer's wit, a poet's sensibility, a storyteller's enthusiasm and a survivor's heart. They have the power to reconnect us to that part of ourselves we need when anything bad happens, that gritty, humored, resilient, unspeakably beautiful spark in the center of each of us that knows only how to lock its jaws and hang on." —**Pam Houston**, author of *Contents May Have Shifted*

"This moving, courageous, honest, and beautifully written account is not about the life of a cancer survivor, but rather of a life defined by living. It was a privilege to read it." —**Nancy Pearl**, NPR commentator and author of *Book Lust: Recommended Reading for Every Mood, Moment, and Reason*

"This book is full of life as the author faces having inflammatory breast cancer and losing her breasts. I love the way she raises questions and makes observations that are intriguing, even occasionally a bit funny, but mostly just the kind of things we'd want to know and wish someone would ask. Plus she writes with skill and panache. Her journey was one I felt compelled to join as she navigates with a unique kind of grace that question "now what!" Simply put I loved this book." —**Sheryl Cotleur**, Buyer, Book Passage

"Staying sane through the insanity of Inflammatory Breast Cancer, letting the mind take you away while poison kills invisible invaders. That is how Katherine walked then ran through prognosis to NED land. Watching friends she had made through breast cancer support groups lose their battles, Katherine never mentions guilt that many women feel when they are still standing as many fall beside them, but you can read between the lines as she takes you through her journey. Going from a mountain top in China to a plastic covered recliner in a chemotherapy room speaks to the reality of the insanity of what life had thrown at Katherine, with Ben by her side wondering what was next. The "next" should be for another book by Katherine Malmo." —**Patti Bradfield**, President of the Inflammatory Breast Cancer Foundation

"Katherine Malmo touches the most tender subject with intimate grace, subtle wit, and piercing honesty. Through the crucible of her own experience, she has forged a life-affirming collection of dazzling stories, lit by hope and sparked by compassion." —**Melanie Rae Thon**, author of *The Voice of the River*

"It's a hell of a thing for anyone to get diagnosed with aggressive breast cancer. Katherine Malmo shares the terror of that—and keeps going. *Who in This Room* puts breast cancer square in its place, right in the middle of life: messy, funny, scary, mundane, over-the-top-emotional life, life filled with fly-fishing and chemo, birthday parties and best friends and breast inserts. Malmo writes with honesty and a hard-won, appealing humor about the gritty and absurd aspects of living with cancer. That this young woman makes it out alive is amazing; by writing about it so gracefully, she lets us take heart from her long haul. Brava, Katherine Malmo. *Who in This Room* is an extraordinary achievement." —**Summer Wood**, author of *Wrecker*

"Lyrical, vivid, a memoirist work of art that glitters as it charges forward and takes your breath away." —**Priscilla Long**, author of *The Writer's Portable Mentor*

"If all stories are in some fashion a quest, Katherine Malmo's story quests toward the triumph of curiosity over fear. 'Sometimes we don't control our own destinies,' Malmo notes near the end of this book, which is her way of shifting the essential question from 'what is it?' to 'don't think I didn't notice' my questions aren't being answered and what are we going to do about this? Employing 'a language as precise as possible,' a recipe recommended by Italo Calvino in his essay 'Exactitude,' with prose welded out of a grab bag of whippet smart observations and searing self-inspection, Malmo guides us from salad spinners to vultures—'these birds didn't cause cancer, but they were attracted to particles in the air that did'—to welding to adoption on her often funny but never self-pitying quest to de-mythologize cancer. It's a quest this reader wouldn't have wanted to miss." —**Scott Driscoll**, Seattle-area author and writing instructor

"A moving, touching memoir about the trauma and triumph of surviving breast cancer. An inspiring read!" —**Nick O'Connell**, author of *On Sacred Ground: The Spirit of Place in Pacific Northwest Literature*, www.thewriters workshop.net.

"*Who In This Room* is an honest, unflinching look at life with cancer, welded into a thing of lyrical beauty. Katherine Malmo, an observant and gifted writer, never misses the irony or insight of a moment, including the one that gives the book its title." —**Erica Bauermeister**, author of *Joy For Beginners*

who
in
this
room:

the realities of cancer,
fish, and demolition

who in this room:

the realities of cancer, fish, and demolition

KATHERINE MALMO

CALYX BOOKS

Publication of this book is made possible in part by the generous support of the Kinsman Foundation, the Meyer Memorial Trust, the Oregon Arts Commission, the National Endowment for the Arts, Christina Bennett in honor of her mother Agnes Glab, Sara Burant and Gene Johnson, and Mary Alice Seville.

Cover by Judy Almazan Stuhmer
Book design by Cheryl McLean

CALYX Books are distributed to the trade through Consortium Book Sales and Distribution, Inc., 1-800-283-3572. CALYX Books are also available through major library distributors, jobbers, and most small press distributors including Baker & Taylor, and Ingram. For personal orders or other information: CALYX Books, PO Box B, Corvallis, OR 97339, (541) 753-9384, FAX (541) 753-0515. www.calyxpress.org.

♾

The paper in this book meets the guidelines for permanence and durability of the Committee on Production Guidelines for Book Longevity of the Council on Library Resources and the minimum requirements of the American National Standard for the Permanence of Paper for Printed Library Materials Z38.48-1984.

Library of Congress Cataloging-in-Publication Data
Malmo, Katherine
    Who in this room : the realities of cancer, fish, and demolition / by Katherine Malmo
        p. cm.
    ISBN 978-0-934971-12-6 (trade paper : alk. paper) —
ISBN 978-0-934971-27-0 (eBook)
    1. Malmo, Katherine. 2. Breast—Cancer—Patients. I. Title.

PS3613.A456W47 2011
814'.6—dc22
                                    2011013363

Printed in the U.S.A.   9 8 7 6 5 4 3 2 1

Dedicated to
Thankful Emily Jane Dade
1977–2007

The infantilizing trope is perplexing.
Certainly men diagnosed with
prostate cancer do not receive
gifts of Matchbox cars.

Barbara Ehrenreich
Harper's Magazine
November 2001

Contents

Publisher's Note

Who in This Room is a work of creative nonfiction. While the events in this book are based in reality, some of the names of characters and places have been changed with respect for privacy. The feelings and decisions described in this book reflect the author's personal experience with illness and do not necessarily speak for the many different journeys of cancer patients and survivors.

For more information, contact the Inflammatory Breast Cancer Foundation at www.eraseibc.com or Young Survivor Coalition at www.youngsurvival.org.

Author's Note

As soon as I completed chemotherapy, I began to write. Some said it was too soon, that I should give myself some time to process and to heal before I laid my life on the page. But I couldn't. The section "Who in This Room" came out fully formed in a single afternoon. It is written in second person and the use of *you* gave me much needed distance from the material, allowing me the freedom to escape the story while telling it. It allowed me to pretend everything that was happening to me was happening to someone else.

From there I wasn't sure where to go. I knew I didn't want to write a memoir. The thought of recounting my whole story was overwhelming. I wanted to capture specific cancer-related moments yet also write about non-cancer life. I wanted to write about travel, fishing, lemon trees, and swimming.

I stayed with second person for the next section, "Permission to Land." As I continued to write through post-chemo radiation and then through my recovery from treatment, I moved into the *he/she* of third person. Using third person still allowed some distance and helped me develop Kate and Ben as characters. By the time I wrote "Made of Metal and Constructed with Fire" and "Reconstruction," I no longer needed the distance. I had somehow acquired the courage to write stories that were me. And I was them.

Permission to Land

Patty says she's having her reconstruction right away because if she is going to die, and she does believe she is dying, then goddamn it, she is going to die with breasts. You haven't even considered reconstruction because while you also believe you are dying, the last place you want to spend your time is in a room with buzzing lights and shiny floors.

Earlier that evening your husband drops you off at the cancer clubhouse for your first young survivor meeting. You pass through the white columns and the red door to the lobby where you wait, your arms crossed for the receptionist. You are apprehensive about all the impending support and the emotions a room full of dying women could evoke. You are afraid someone will try to hold your hand or leap from behind the ficus to hug you.

You are directed to a large room that doubles as a kids' playroom with trees, bunnies, and rainbows painted on the walls. Ten short-haired or bald women are sitting in a circle of mismatched couches and armchairs. You choose a spot on the end of a couch, cross your legs, and lean your elbow into the armrest.

For your introduction you say your nausea is strong and that you are barely eating and when chemotherapy is over, you'll have a mastectomy. The surgeons said your left breast had to go, that had already been decided, but what happens to your right breast, which shows no sign of cancer, is up to you. That was when you decided it was time to hear what these women have to say.

After Patty talks about reconstruction, Martha says she sees the same surgeon. Martha calls her the *Versace of mastectomy* because she does such beautiful work. *Tiny, straight scars, no lumps or bumps.* Martha tugs at the loose ends of her head scarf and says her friend's scar is sloppy, messy, poor work. You read that patients of doctors who perform more than fifty breast surgeries per year are much less likely to have a recurrence.

Gradually the conversation moves on to treatment protocols and the management of symptoms. There is some talk of death and a few tears but there is no unnecessary hugging. There is no singing or hand holding. There is no counselor with crayons telling you to draw out your feelings. Mostly you talk about things like the daily Neupogen shots that boost your white blood cell production and whether you like it better in the morning, noontime, or evening; in the arm, thigh, or abdomen; and which family member administers them best or if you do it yourself.

You like these women. You take a full page of notes on drug and doctor names. While you listen to the last bits of advice, your eyes rest on a pile of games stacked in the corner. You think that if you could just get the right medication and the right surgeon and if you could just choose the right solution for your right breast, then maybe everything would be alright.

You didn't like the first surgeon you met because she gave you the bad news. You liked the second but decided she didn't have enough experience. A week later, you meet Versace.

When she says you need a mastectomy on the left side, you say, "I'm struggling with the fate of my right breast."

She checks her watch and says, "You have a twenty percent chance of developing a new primary tumor."

"What would you do?" you ask.

She looks at her watch again. "I'm sorry, I didn't schedule this much time."

You've heard she's always on time. She is precise. You aren't looking for a therapist; you're looking for a cutter. She is exactly what you want. She tape records your first meeting and the only tape deck you own is in your car. When you drive to the store to buy more eggs, you listen again to what she said about your impending surgery.

"The skin is involved," she says. "We will have to take the skin."

You wonder if you will have enough to cover the hole.

Three weeks later, in the heat of summer, when you've completed six of your twenty-seven weekly chemotherapy infusions, you feel like you're filled with cold water and take a hot bath. You picture yourself without breasts and imagine a smudge made with an old pencil eraser where they used to be. When you look closely, you notice tiny wrinkles on the skin near your nipple. They are cancer cells marching from your left breast to your right; you just know it's spreading.

The next day when you see your oncologist, she leans forward and looks at your chest with a magnifying glass. "I think they're stretch marks," she says.

You wonder why you would have stretch marks. You've never had children and consider that perhaps your oncologist doesn't have any idea what she is talking about and that maybe you should find another one.

"Okay, we'll do another MRI," she says finally, sitting back on her stool.

Over the weekend, you wait for the report and worry about the spread of your tumor. It's 5.2 cm of the most aggressive form of cancer. The full-body scan done two months ago showed there were no other malignant lumps—that it had not spread to your bones, liver, or lungs—but you know there could be clusters of cells too small to detect.

This tumor is not a virus, not something you caught; these cancer cells are not foreign intruders. This is your own creation—a cluster of cells that developed abnormally, multiplying beyond your control. Perhaps your immune system was overtaxed. When treatment is over, you want every bit of energy to go toward fighting stray cancer cells, not dealing with cancer that may or may not be taking hold in your other breast.

On your thirty-second birthday, over a cup of onion confit at your favorite restaurant, you say to your husband, "I think the right breast has to go." Then, "How'd you end up with a bald, breastless wife at the age of thirty-two?"

He says, "Don't worry, Babe, I've always been more of an ass man myself."

You try to smile but instead you cry. Tears drip into your soup.

He raises his glass of wine. "How about we buy a new, sportier car for your birthday?"

You buy the cancer/birthday car the next day.

Your husband lists the old car for sale. One rainy night you meet the buyers, a young couple with a baby, in a parking lot. While they install the car seat, you look one last time through the glove box and under the armrest until you're sure it's empty. The buyers hand over the cash, and you and your husband drive away without looking back.

You put a bumper sticker on your new car that says *What if the hokey pokey IS what it's all about?*

You are driving the cancer/birthday car to your next support group meeting when your oncologist calls to say the scan showed the tumor had shrunk. You smile and think perhaps this doctor does know something about cancer and chemotherapy and that you will stay with her for now. But you still see danger everywhere and you know that some tumors don't show up on MRIs.

This time the group meets in the room with the unlit fireplace and a tea candle burning on a table in the center. Allison introduces herself, "Hi, my name is Allison, and, yes, my left nipple still points at the floor." After chemotherapy, mastectomy, radiation, and a hysterectomy, Allison had reconstruction—some tram-flap something-or-other where they sewed her abdominal muscles to her chest. "I go back to correct the floor-pointing nipple next month," she says. "I hope the recovery is quick because I still can't hold Noah on my lap. He's only three but he's a big boy."

Kathy says her mother and aunt both had breast cancer. Already a survivor of thyroid cancer, she was thinking of having a prophylactic mastectomy before she was diagnosed at the age of thirty-six.

"My breasts were small and lumpy," she says. "I'd had three biopsies that year. The tumor was hard to find. If my cancer came back, I wasn't sure we'd be able to catch it in the early stages." She had her bilateral mastectomy a year ago and her small prosthetic breasts hang low on her chest. "I miss my breasts," she says. "It would have been nice to keep one."

Before they go home all the women jam into the bathroom to look at Allison's new breasts. She pulls up her shirt.

"Can I touch them?" someone asks.

"They look so real."

Everyone giggles.

All you can see is the scar that runs through Allison's belly button from one hip bone to the other, and you wonder if she needed those abdominal muscles for something else.

As summer changes to fall, you change chemotherapy drugs. The nausea disappears but now you have trouble walking. In spite of the joint pain, or maybe because of it, you go to a fundraising walk. A reporter asks why you are there. You know he wants you to say something like: *No one should have to face cancer alone* or *Together we're going to beat this damn cancer*, or some other rah-rah bullshit but the only response you can think of is: *I'm worried I won't have enough skin to cover the holes where my breasts used to be.* Instead you tell him you don't want to be on television.

At the next meeting Ginger says she wanted to get a hooker for her husband for Christmas. "'Cuz, for god's sake, the man needed to get laid, and after six months of chemotherapy, I certainly wasn't in the mood."

You're thinking about starting your own surly survivor club, and decide she should be the second member—or maybe a co-founder. You recognize Ginger as a special friend, one you know you will keep forever.

She's a few weeks ahead of you in treatment. When she discovered her lump, she was living in Alaska where the dark winters made her depressed and sick. She wanted to move but didn't because her husband and two children are Native American Alaskans. Since her diagnosis, she's relocated the family to Seattle. Ella is eight and Henry is five, and they miss the snow.

You visit Ginger's house one day for tea. She's wearing a knit cap with a flower drooping over her ear. You wonder how someone so small could have hidden a tumor so large for so long. You spend hours in her living room, where the eagle feathers hang straight down from the ceiling, talking about the merits of unilateral versus bilateral.

"If I do both," she says, pulling her bare foot up onto the couch, "maybe sometimes I can go out without prosthetics and just be flat-chested."

You sit sideways and set your arm on the back of the couch. You hadn't thought of that. "If I keep one, I'll have some sensation. I hear that once they're gone, you don't ever get the feeling back."

"More water?" She pours hot water into the mug resting on your thigh. "But even if you do both," she says, "you can still have a recurrence in the remaining tissue around the scar, but I guess it's less likely."

"My breast tissue is so fibrous," you say, "mammograms don't work well for me. I don't know if we'd catch my recurrence early enough. And my immune system... It can only take so much. If it isn't fighting cancer in my breast, then maybe it will be better at fighting cancer in the other parts of my body."

"It's not like they're vital organs anyway," Ginger says.

"We can live without them," you say. It comes out sounding like a question.

It snows on the day of Ginger's bilateral mastectomy. You walk your dog, scraping your own path along the sidewalk, past Ginger's dark house. The branches of the hemlock in the corner of her yard are weighed down by wet snow. They could break. You can't just wait and watch to see what will happen. You pull the end of one branch and the snow slips into a pile on the ground. Then you reach inside, grab the trunk and shake. You shake and shake and eventually the snow falls from the tree dropping onto your arm, your head. It slips inside your collar.

One winter day, after you've completed chemotherapy, you decide to go shopping. Buying new bras seems like an odd thing to do, but your old bras' straps rub against the Port-a-Cath that sticks out of your chest, and besides, you can wear these bras someday with your prosthetics. While measuring your ribcage, the saleswoman says, "You're one of those enviable women who is skinny but has large breasts."

You are not able to resist saying, "Not for long." But you say it with a smile and laugh. She disappears into the back and another saleswoman rings up your purchase. You feel like yelling, *I was just kidding!*

Then you go to the cosmetics counter to buy a new blush and put some color in your chemo-gray cheeks and an eyeliner to define your brow-less, lash-less eyes. You ask the makeup artist if you should line your lower eyelid.

"Depends," she says. "Some women do, and some don't."

"Yeah," you say. "But what do you recommend for someone without eyelashes?"

It's times like this, when your reign of terror sweeps through the retail world, that while you hate being bald, you appreciate its outward expression of your sickness. If it helps people be a bit nicer to you, then you are grateful.

You prepare for your surgery by filling the fridge with nutritious healing whole foods—kale, kohlrabi, lentils, artichoke hearts. It feels like you're preparing for a snow storm, a hurricane, or some other natural disaster. You nest like your pregnant friends. You use the vacuum. Your husband doesn't know what to expect, but he doesn't expect a clean house.

Your sister flies in from San Francisco. At 5:00 a.m. you get dressed. You wear sweat bottoms and a button-down shirt that you'll be able to put on when it is time to come home. Your husband and your sister take you to the hospital. After changing into a robe, you follow the nurse into a big cold room with bright lights and shiny floors, and she asks you to lie down on a table shaped like your body, with arms and legs. Versace looks like a clown in her black and white checkered hat. She smiles and asks, "How are you?" And it seems like she means it.

"I'm alright," you say.

She is shining. This is where she wanted to be when she looked at her watch that day.

"I just need to..." The anesthesiologist untangles a mess of yellow cables near your head. "I just need to get these cords untangled and I'll give you a little something to help you..."

You wake up floating in a bubble of hot air.

"Are you feeling any pain?" a nurse with long brown hair pulled back in a ponytail asks.

You aren't sure, but know enough to say yes. Your husband appears, but you are unable to take your eyes off the Hello Kitty faces on the nurse's scrubs. Hello Kitty dances all around.

"I loooovvee Hello Kitty," you say, laughing at her sweet, mouthless face. "Can I have some more of that good medicine?" you ask, reaching for her sleeve. As she pushes a syringe into your IV, you remember the Hello Kitty haiku postcard you saw last week at a gift shop.

"Pink bird descending," you mumble.

"What?" Your husband leans close.

"Control tower to kitty." You laugh.

As you are wheeled away, instead of saying thank you, you say, "Permission to land."

You're taken to a private room, which is good because you don't like to share. You spend what seems like hours sleeping, hooked up to a machine that gives you morphine every fifteen minutes. Your husband, mother, and sister watch.

You wake up to find the head of the bed elevated thirty degrees, inflatable braces massaging your legs to keep stroke-inducing clots from forming, and two warm ice packs resting on your chest. You tell the nurse you need more ice. They aren't cold. When she feels them, she looks at you funny but comes back with fresh ice. You call her again an hour later.

"There must be something wrong with these packs," you say.

"They feel cold to me," she replies. She picks them up and when you hear the ice rustling, you realize the packs are cold—you just can't feel them.

Three plastic drain tubes, one for each lost breast and one for the fifteen lymph nodes they removed from your armpit, run under your skin, around where your breasts used to be, and out little holes in the middle of your ribcage, down to bulbs that sit next to your hips on the mattress.

Versace stops by to tell you the surgery went "very well." Her smile is smug and almost shy. "The pathology won't be ready for a week," she says softly. You flinch when she moves to pat your arm.

At 10:00 p.m. your husband offers to stay in the room or in a nearby hotel but he looks tired and you send him home. You can't sleep and ask the nurse for a sleeping pill. She says she needs the doctor's signature and she can't get it before the shift change. You ask the new nurse. You ask her again. It's 3:00 a.m., your legs are strapped to a machine. You're still connected to an IV you haven't used in hours, three drains are hanging from your ribs, two warm ice packs lie across your chest, and the head of your bed is elevated thirty degrees. The tears are just about to start when the nurse finally arrives with a tiny pill in a tiny cup.

At 6:00 a.m. a new nurse wakes you to clean your drains and empty the fluid. When she removes the ice packs, you see the surgeon's work for the first time. Each side has a thin strip about an inch tall and six inches long that runs horizontally across your chest, which is encased in plastic wrap. You are surprised how small the bandages are and how small the holes must have been.

That afternoon you return home and sleep, finally, without a sleeping pill. It's a stiff and controlled sleep on your back with the drains at your sides, and when you wake up the pain along your chest, sides, and armpits is dull and aching. You get up to clean the drains and realize you left the specimen cup, used to measure the fluid, at the hospital. You send your sister to the drugstore to buy something that will measure small amounts of fluid. She comes back with a

Winnie the Pooh baby bottle. Three times a day, every day, Winnie helps measure the bloody fluid that your nodes are no longer there to collect.

Two days after surgery, even though you still don't have any hair to wash, you decide to shower and tie loops in the ends of a piece of kitchen string. You hang the drains from the loops and run the string over your neck. In the shower you lift your arm just enough to squeeze in a razor to shave the prickly stubble and realize your armpit has moved. It angles onto your chest. You can see the skin is pulled tight and that there was barely enough to cover the hole.

You start referring to your drains as your babies. The bulbs are too big to fit in your pant pockets so you wear your hooded sweatshirt with big pockets every day as you carry them around like a high school home economics project. They are always with you, always in need of care. When your husband finally takes down the Christmas lights, you find a gutter hook on the coffee table. It's perfect. You take three and hook your babies to your belt loops.

With Winnie's help you continue to clean the drains three times a day. They are supposed to be in for ten to fourteen days. After seventeen days, two drains produce less than thirty cc's each and come out. The third drain's production hits seventy cc's with no sign of slowing. The skin is angry and red where the tube enters your body. You wrap an Ace bandage around your torso to keep the tube from moving. You spend days sitting still because Ginger told you it might slow fluid production.

After twenty-one days, it takes all your self-control to keep from yanking the tube out yourself. Pain shoots up your torso. At your appointment, Versace doesn't meet your eyes. Her tone is short. She says she doesn't recommend taking it out, but ultimately it is your choice.

When she pulls out the twelve inches of tubing that have been living under your skin for three weeks, you think it will hurt, but all you feel is sweet relief. You prepare for massive swelling from all the undrained fluid, but two days later the nurse and her giant syringe remove only ten cc's.

Your friend brings flowers, white lilies in a green vase that you set in the middle of the coffee table. She takes a sip of tea and asks, "How do you think you're dealing with it?"

You pull your tea bag back and forth across your cup.

Then she asks, "How has the experience changed you?"

You are unable to give her an answer, but a week later you call and tell her that now you give your dog the table scraps you used to throw away.

Carmen started going to support group before you, but only starts speaking at your first post-mastectomy meeting. She was diagnosed with pre-cancer three years ago and opted for a mastectomy. She found a lump near her scar two years later when she was nine months pregnant.

"I asked my doctor to induce on a Tuesday," she says, "because I knew I would hear I had cancer on Wednesday. I didn't want to be diagnosed on my baby's birthday."

Since the lump was on her chest wall and also in her remaining breast tissue, the doctors couldn't tell her if it was a local or metastatic recurrence. The doctors couldn't tell her if she was stage II or stage IV.

"I did everything I could," she says. "I had the mastectomy, but there are no guarantees, only expensive tests with high rates of false negatives."

Your post-op appointment is scheduled for the day after support group. The MRI you had after chemotherapy showed only a four millimeter spec of tumor remaining. You hope the surgical pathology will show that the spec was scar tissue and that really you had a "complete pathologic recovery" even before surgery.

You can hear your doctor's voice through the door as you look straight out the window to the wet parking lot.

She comes in and says, "Pathology shows the removal of a 2.2 centimeters mass from your left breast..."

You gasp and drop your head into your hands and hear nothing more as you think about what you will say to your oncologist to convince her to give you more chemotherapy because twenty-seven doses obviously wasn't enough. Maybe, you think, you could switch to Patty's doctor. He'd let you have more chemo.

While you are getting your parking validated at the front desk, your husband reads the pathology report. He has some questions and you go back into an exam room.

"Is the mass dead?" he asks.

"Yes," Versace says. "The mass is a skeleton with a few scattered cancer cells remaining. Your nodes were all negative. I don't like to use the word remission—it implies the cancer will come back. But you are officially NED—no evidence of disease."

At home you study the report, looking up words online that you don't know. It is good news, but you feel heavy, tired. You should celebrate. Instead you pull up your hood and walk the dog among the naked trees that line the street and think about the pathology report that described how each breast was cut into eighteen different pieces. You follow the dog as he wraps his leash around a telephone pole and think about how Versace must have sliced your breasts off whole, to keep the tissue intact, so the pathologist could dissect them.

You don't feel like celebrating. You didn't gain anything. After losing your appetite, your hair, many of your white blood cells, and your breasts, the good news is that it's less likely that anything else will be taken away.

You picture your tissue lying in a plastic garbage can in a sterile room with shiny floors and wonder what they will do with your breasts now that their work is done. Maybe you should have kept one. You wonder if you should ask for them back and bury them under the lilac near the cat. But then you wonder how you could ever sell a house that had your breasts buried in the yard.

When you think about selling your house, you realize you never took the surgeon's appointment recording from the tape deck of your old car. Someday, someone you don't know will press play and your grief will be out in the world without you, like your missing tissue.

You're a few weeks out of surgery, and your hair is almost long enough to go without a scarf when you decide it's time to buy new breasts. You've been to this store before looking for special support stockings for your ninety-eight-year-old grandmother and remember the pressed glass bowl filled with peppermint candies next to the register. You choose a pair of attachable breasts that you call "stick-ons." They look like what you used to have, and you wonder if it would have been difficult to match a real breast to a fake one.

While you wait for your new breasts to arrive, the store loans you a pair. They are a *C* cup, smooth and cool to touch and heavy in your hand like a bag of marbles. They are fair-colored, but mismatched, and the nipples are always slightly erect. They smell like someone else.

"I'm wearing someone else's breasts," you tell your husband over a pork chop dinner. He murmurs an acknowledgement. "No, really, I'm wearing *someone else's breasts*." And this time you reach into your shirt to retrieve the loaner breast, push your hand across the table, and hold it up to his nose.

He swallows, sniffs, and says, "All I can smell is your perfume."

You say, "That's exactly my point! It's not *my* perfume!"

It smells like an old woman, who you assume died and her husband or children donated her breast to the cause. You take the smelly breast into the shower and wash it with your soap. But the stink stays.

At the next group you meet Natalie, who found a lump while breastfeeding her ten-day-old son. She was diagnosed stage IV one week later. Her son is now five and she's been on some kind of chemotherapy for nearly his whole life. She stopped covering her bald head long ago, and the chemo-induced nerve damage is so extensive that she has no feeling in her feet. She believes the cure is imminent.

You talk about your fears of recurrence. While flipping through the newspaper insert looking at coupons, she says, "You just deal with it because you have to. Life goes on."

The sun is out when you drive downtown to pick up your new breasts. The dog hangs his head out the open window, and on the drive home you think you see your old car parked on the street. The people who bought it live a few hours north, but maybe they're visiting someone in the city. Maybe you could get your cassette. You make a U-turn, stop across the street, and pull a piece of paper from your purse to write a note. *Did you buy this car last fall? Was there a cassette in the deck? If so, please call me. I'd really like it back. I don't feel right without it.* You write your phone number and sign your name.

It's rush hour and cars whiz past your door. You wait for a break and when you step out into the street your dog starts to bark. As you cross, you look over your shoulder to see him running back and forth, over the seats, the length of the car. When you reach the other curb, you realize the license plate is different. When you look inside, the seats are cloth, not leather. You feel silly thinking you could get it back. You crumple the note in your pocket as you step off the curb. The dog puts his paws up on the window and barks. He's worried you're out there alone. He's telling you to be careful. You yell to him. You tell him it's okay, that you're coming back, that everything will be fine, just fine, and you believe it because you are looking both ways and walking quickly and you know that even if a car arrives before you get to the other side, you are doing everything you can.

No One Said Anything About Corn

Three years before Kate found her lump, she and her husband arrived in southern China to hike the Yangtze River's Tiger Leaping Gorge. The cherry trees were in bloom, and blossoms blew across a cobblestone square to a bench where a man leaned in and talked to a woman in a blue apron.

"He's looking for the perfect towels," Kate said, playing their game. "White, with bumblebees embroidered along the bottom."

"Eats pudding pops in bed," Ben said, knowing this was ridiculous because no one made pudding pops anymore. "Sleeps alone."

Inside a tea house, a tape recorder sat on an empty table repeating an English conversation—"Hello, I would like a reservation for dinner... for how many... six, please..." They read a wall papered with notes from other hikers. *Too wet in September,* one said. *Leave early. Follow the red arrows. When in doubt, take the well-worn path.* When the manager stepped around the bar, she gave them a hand-drawn map of the three-day hike and told them there was no need for a guide. A group would only slow them down.

She pointed to a section on the map and said, "You, maybe you hike in eight hour but Chinese, Chinese no hike in eight hour."

Kate pictured a cluster of matching turquoise baseball hats following a woman with a bullhorn and triangular turquoise flag.

That night Kate and Ben re-packed their bags for the three-day trek so they could each carry a gallon of water, a bag of trail mix, and a change of clothes. They planned to sleep and eat in guest houses along the route. When they climbed into bed, it was hot and their window opened onto an alley where a couple threw harsh Mandarin words over the music of a pan flute. The woman started to cry. Ben wrapped his arms around Kate and pushed his nose into the back of her neck.

"Never puts the lid on the toothpaste," Ben said.

"Spells her name with an 'i' not an 'e.'"

The next morning in a crowded bus on a muddy road, Kate glanced over her shoulder and past a basket of flustered chickens to catch Ben's eye as he stood holding two bars, bracing himself for the long ride ahead.

Three years later, at home in Seattle, cherry blossoms piled up like leaves along the edges of the sidewalk while Kate and Ben walked their dog toward the neighbor's house that usually had free stuff in the yard. An old lady trimmed her lawn with hand shears.

"Eats possum meat and gummy worms," Ben said. "Exclusively. But never together."

As they approached, a black cat puffed and the old lady said, "I think your doggie is afraid of my kitty."

"I think I'm afraid of your kitty," Kate mumbled.

The old lady, still hunched over, walked to Kate and said, "There's free cake next door. It's good."

They turned the corner to find a big white cake sitting on a stool next to a cardboard sign that said "free." It was a three-layered number with coconut frosting. Kate didn't eat cake, but Ben took a piece.

"See," he said, mouth full. "Not all free stuff is bad." Ben had an attraction to roadside furniture.

They walked on to a park with a view of Mount Rainier reflecting the pink setting sun before returning home in the dark and curling up in bed.

The next morning Kate wiped the steam from the bathroom mirror and noticed one of her nipples looked swollen and different from the other. At first, she thought it hadn't adjusted to the cool air. She gave it a few minutes. But it didn't adjust and when her hair was dry, she started poking around. She noticed that her whole left breast, not just the nipple, was bigger than the right. She hadn't been doing self-exams, but it didn't take long to find the quarter-sized hard spot, like a tendon or a muscle stretched tight, just above her left nipple.

They rode the bus for four hours, then walked past the brick schoolhouse and the untethered horse to a footpath hidden in the brush. Soon they came to an unmarked *Y* in the trail that everyone said was well marked with red spray-painted arrows. They chose the wider branch that switch-backed up the hill, through terraced rice fields and past a water buffalo whose horns parted like hair in the middle of its forehead.

Two hours later a Chinese man in a purple and red sweatshirt ran out of a rice field waving his arms.

"Sings Devo to the cows," Ben said, panting, hands on his hips.

"Raises champion cock fighters," she said. "Makes trophies from cereal boxes."

The farmer spoke Mandarin and talked with his hands. Perhaps they were headed the wrong way. Kate pulled the map from her pocket; she was sure these switchbacks were the section called *28 bends*. Kate looked at the farmer and pointed down the road, the way they'd come, and raised her hands, shoulders, and eyebrows to form the universal gesture for confusion. The farmer shook his head no and called over his teenage son.

"Twenty dollar," the farmer said, "for lead way."

"Oh, no thanks," Ben said, waving them away.

Kate and Ben soldiered on up the hill, assuring themselves they were headed in the right direction and the farmer just wanted to make a buck.

"If this was twenty-eight bends," Ben said, "why have we already counted thirty? And shouldn't we have seen some other hikers on the trail? Or at least a few arrows?"

They'd only been hiking for two hours but their burning thighs made it feel like forever.

A week after she found the hard spot, Ben caught Kate's hand with his to slow her down as they walked along the sidewalk strewn with blossoms to her doctor's office. She'd had the mammograms, the sonograms, and finally the needle core biopsy. The technicians had been cagey—no one would say anything for sure. Finally, after a week of testing, it was time to get the results.

They'd hardly taken their seats when the nurse called Kate's name and they followed her past the scale without stopping for Kate's weight. Her blood pressure was not taken. She did not change into a robe. Inside the exam room a woman's anatomy drawing hung next to a rack of brochures for diseases Kate didn't have. On the back of the door was a hand-drawn map of the room identifying where every piece of furniture belonged. As far as Kate could tell, everything was in its place.

Ben and Kate sat next to each other, arms crossed, with their backs to the wall. Ben stood and walked to the window, scratching his ear with his thumbnail.

"Nothing," he said, turning to face her. "I'm sure it's nothing."

"I know," she said, pulling the hood of her sweatshirt around her neck.

Ben leaned his back against the sill and said, "You're fine, right? They have to bring everyone in."

"I just wish, god," she sighed. "I wish this was over."

"Standard procedure," he said.

"I feel like I've been waiting forever."

They continued to trudge uphill for three more hours, switching back and forth, past forty bends.

"Maybe the mapmaker didn't count the little bends," Kate suggested. "Or maybe the switchback formation changed recently."

They didn't pass any red arrows or other hikers. Ben stopped. Sat on a boulder. Took a drink. Kate gave him a handful of peanuts and pulled the raisins out of the trail mix for herself. Below, the Yangtze sliced a path between two mountains.

"Do you think that's the spot?" she asked. Chinese legend said a tiger, pursued by hunters, leapt ninety feet from one bank to the other.

"Doesn't look like such a big leap from here," Ben said.

Kate tapped her lips with the tips of her fingers and considered their next move. The trail was supposed to be covered with red arrows.

"Maybe we should go back and look for a *Y* in the trail," she said.

"We've been hiking for five hours," he said.

"Maybe we took the wrong path back at the beginning, you know, when we went left, right before the buffalo."

"It's dinner time. We know we're headed the right direction, we're still following the river, the right trail has to be here somewhere." He sloshed water through his teeth. "It would take us five hours to hike down to that *Y*. It will be dark by then and where will we sleep? We'll still have a six-hour hike to the Tea Horse Guesthouse. By then it will be 1:00 a.m. and we'll be hiking in the dark."

Finally Kate agreed to see what was around the next bend. Just past a lone tree, windblown and gnarled, they could see their trail descend into a field of corn. Corn. Their map didn't say anything about corn, or peas, or beans, or vegetables of any kind.

When Ben turned back to the window, the usual small rip he got from leaning on co-workers' doors and catching his shirttail on the hooked handles stuck out from under his fleece jacket.

Kate scratched her breast with the hand hidden under her crossed arm. The day she noticed her retracted nipple, it had itched as if it was reminding her it was there, reminding her to see a doctor. She'd returned to the bathroom mirror four times, unable to believe the deformity was permanent.

There was a soft knock and they both turned to look.

"Yes, yes, come in."

The doctor, still in her green surgical scrubs, stepped around the open door. Ben sat and wrapped his fingers around the armrests.

Eats potato chips inside her sandwich, Kate thought.

The doctor wasn't smiling. She sat on her rolling stool next to a desk with a picture of a little boy dressed as a tiger and pulled off her green cap, exciting a crop of small broken hairs around her forehead.

Slices sandwiches diagonally.

The doctor opened a file and clicked her pen twice. She sighed.

Hates mayonnaise.

She looked at Kate directly through her frameless glasses.

Butters both pieces of bread.

She smelled like cherry-flavored cough drops.

Cuts off the crusts for the tiger.

"I don't have good news," she said. "The tumor is malignant."

Kate stared past the doctor to the tiger. She pulled on the patch of skin between her index finger and thumb.

Kate caught up to Ben and grabbed his arm just above the elbow. It was their sign for *I need help.* He often used it when they were with her family, and by the time they left holiday dinners her arm was usually bruised and sore. She knew she could have just told him she was worried, but there was something more intimate about touching that place above the elbow and the concern in his eyes when they met hers.

"I know," he said. "Me too."

That cornfield wasn't right. Kate's legs ached and her shoulder was rubbed raw from her pack. They passed a downed pine tree with an excavated root base that loomed over their heads, and Kate wondered what brought this tree, and not any of its neighbors, down.

The evening sun was already casting long shadows and Kate slapped at a mosquito on her forearm. They stopped on a precipice overlooking the cornfield. It would be dark soon and even Kate agreed they were committed to this path. If they turned back now, they would be hiking all night in the dark without headlamps or flashlights.

"You see that," Ben said pointing down the hill. "I think it's a trail. Maybe that's where we're supposed to be."

As they continued down the path toward the field, loose soil rolled under Kate's feet. She slid down the steep incline on her back, trying to grab roots of trees, branches, and shrubs as they slid by. She came to a stop, covered in dirt, only when she hit the first row of stalks.

Kate leaned forward, put her forearms on her knees, and continued to pull on the patch of skin between her thumb and index finger. She recognized the metallic taste of fear in her mouth from the few times she'd been truly lost.

"Are you sure?" Ben asked, turning his head to look at the doctor. "I'm just...surprised."

Kate felt Ben's hand on her back, fingers extended.

"The nurse said," Ben continued, "that there was an eighty-five percent chance it was benign. And no family history. And she's only thirty-one."

Names her children after seasons, she thought.

"Really?" Ben said.

"How do I know this isn't a mistake?" Kate asked.

"Will she need chemotherapy?" Ben inhaled.

Outside a siren wailed.

Kate covered her eyes with fingers that smelled like Ben's burned cinnamon raisin bread that she'd pulled from the toaster. Tears dripped into her palms. The doctor said it was treatable.

"Will she have surgery?" The vein up the middle of Ben's forehead looked like it would burst.

The doctor handed her a computer print-out list of appointments. A mammogram for her other breast, an MRI, and three doctor's appointments—surgeon, medical oncologist, and radiologist—were highlighted with an antifreeze-green pen. She said it depended on what the scans showed and the oncologists said.

Kate took a tissue, slouched in her chair, and tore it into long ribbons in her lap.

Ben took her hand and leaned back. A sharp exhale. A shake of his head. "Shouldn't we get it out?" he asked.

"As soon as we can," the doctor said.

"The appointment with the surgeon isn't for four days. That's a long time."

"It's aggressive, yes, but five days...five days will be okay."

Kate exhaled and reached for her handbag that was hiding under the chair.

The doctor wrote in her file.

Kate turned to Ben and, reaching for that spot just above his elbow, asked, "Am I going to die?"

"Breast cancer treatment has come a long way," the doctor said without looking up.

Kate and Ben tried to cut a straight trail down through the stalks. But they were in over their heads and, like swimmers in a lake, straight was difficult to discern. Ben found a rock and jumped high, hoping to see the end of the field. Kate pushed her way through the stalks, untangling her bag from the leaves and the joints that would soon hold ears of corn. They needed to hurry. Kate had read somewhere that corn grows three centimeters a day. They were growing right then, making each moment harder than the last. Ben jumped from the boulder while Kate pushed through, hoping that if they continued they'd find their place on the map or a few red arrows to point the way.

Matched

The house sat squarely on the lot, the backyard enclosed with a tall cedar fence that kept the dog contained most of the time. A thirty-foot robinia tree with tiny oval leaves leaned over the fence from the neighbor's yard, partly shading the garden beds the couple built together two weeks earlier. Kate had found and printed the instructions. Ben had gone to the hardware store. She dug. He cut. They both carried dirt, one wheelbarrow at a time until the beds were full. Then they covered the garden with black plastic to warm the soil in preparation for spring season planting.

The glass door to the kitchen was open, and an unusually warm wind pushed it gently against the stopper. There was no screen. A fly banged against a window. She hated the bang of a screen more than the buzz of the occasional bug.

Wearing her favorite orange-and-pink-striped pajama bottoms and an old orange tank top, she set two plates of scrambled eggs and fried potatoes on the table. His plate also had toast, which he buttered.

She looked out the doorway at the neighbor's green robinia.

"Remember how it looked last fall," she said, smiling and pointing to the tree with the tines of her fork. "The tree, you remember? The gold leaves matched the color of the house perfectly. It was like they belonged together."

"I don't know what kind of moron paints his house gold." He pushed up his black-framed glasses with the knuckle of his index finger.

"Oh, it was beautiful," she said slowly. "They must have painted it in the fall. To match the tree. They probably just took one of those pretty little leaves into the paint store."

"I mean, I hate homeowner's associations but that, right there, is the best argument I've ever seen. Someone's got to keep people from painting their houses gold."

"They have invasive roots. Robinia. I hope it isn't near their sewer line."

"Would serve them right." He dropped his fork and it hit the plate.

"God. You sure are in a bad mood." She turned a page of *The New York Times*.

"Guess I'm just irritated. Irritated we're talking about the neighbor's house." He gestured toward the door with a shift of the eyes and a slight tilt of the head. "It's just...you know, I know you don't want to talk about it, but I need to leave for the clinic soon. To give my...you know, jerk-off into a cup or whatever I'm supposed to do. But I need to be there in the next hour if we want to do it."

"I liked the doctor—what did she call herself? A fertility *preservationist*?" she asked, tucking her hair behind her ear. "I think she'd do a good job. Nice of her to get us in so quickly."

"And if we don't..." He raised his eyebrows. "If we don't do it, then you need to make an appointment for surgery, like, tomorrow, right?"

"But that nurse was a bitch," she said and tried to move her legs from under her chair but his were stretched into her space.

A crow hopped across the roof, pecking at the shingles. It sounded like someone was knocking on the door. The dog barked twice.

"I know," she said, dropping her shoulders and her hands into her lap.

He wrapped his hands around his cup and watched her, waiting for her to continue.

"I thought we decided to plant seeds," she said, looking toward the box of starts that sat on the back deck. "I thought vegetable seeds and flowers. I thought we would plant some flowers."

He swished water through his teeth like mouthwash and swallowed. "Too late now. Seeds need to germinate. And there won't be enough room for flowers."

"Just need a little fertilizer," she said, bringing a bite of potato to her mouth. Then, with her mouth full, "Better to start them ourselves and make sure they don't have any bugs or caterpillars or slugs. God, I hate slugs." She swallowed. "You know, I read that those little black slugs that ate the leaves on the daphne out front aren't even native to the Northwest. They're like French or European or something. I can't remember. The big banana slugs, that eat dead stuff like fallen leaves, they're the locals. Figures."

"I've wondered," he said, biting into his toast, "since Dad died so young, if maybe I shouldn't have children. I mean, biological."

She bit the end of her thumbnail and looked up at the wrought-iron chandelier where three of the five bulbs were burned out. She stared, not blinking, trying to hold the tears in her eyes.

"There are lots of kids," he said, leaning forward over his plate. "Maybe someday when your treatment is over, we could get two. Siblings. I bet we could do it before your thirty-fifth birthday." He said fifth like *fif*, dropping the *th*.

"I always thought I would be pregnant. I'd be big and waddle and, you know, put one hand on the small of my back for balance."

"I know," he said, waving a fly from his plate.

"That I'd squeeze your hand so tight that we'd both be screaming in the delivery room. It'd just be the two of us. Maybe my mom too."

"No way, not your mom."

"Thought I'd breast-feed."

"It's too risky," he said, tilting his head a bit to the right. "I mean just getting the eggs."

She swallowed a sip of almond milk.

"You remember that toast Todd gave for Mom? At her birthday party?" she said, running her index finger around the rim of her glass. "At the end. He said her children were her life's work and greatest accomplishment. Her life's work. To think that I'm someone's life's work. That's big. Huge, really."

"Yeah." He tapped his nails against his glass. "But the estrogen. I mean those shots will just feed the tumor. So giving you more, extra? I don't care what the doctor says. It just doesn't seem right."

"What do you think being pregnant without breasts would be like? Would I still make milk? Where would it go?"

"Just doesn't seem right, you know?"

She leaned back in her chair and rubbed the thumb of one hand along the palm of the other. "Do you know which one is the lifeline? I bought Tami this palm reading book in college and it said I had a short lifeline. We thought it was funny."

"Okay, so say we do delay your treatment, and she freezes and makes her, I mean our, embryos."

She rolled up the corner of her placemat and said, "Potatoes need salt."

"Then what?"

"Then they will taste better."

"Stop it," he said loud enough for the dog to lift his head. "Then, after all that chemotherapy, even if you do get pregnant or we have those embryos planted and they do take, then you'd be filled with estrogen, and feeding all those left-over cancer cells, right? Doesn't seem like a good idea, you know?"

"Maybe when I turn thirty-three," she said, "then I'll be done with treatment. Maybe when my age is symmetrical, my life will straighten out. Maybe then."

"Potatoes need salt," she said again, handing him the shaker.

As he took the shaker he knocked over his coffee. "Damn it!" he said, pushing away from the table. "Damn it!"

The black coffee slipped over the edge of the table and streamed onto the floor. He absorbed the liquid with his white napkin, keeping the dog away with his other hand. When he was finished, he salted his potatoes and set the shaker on the table with a bang. Then he leaned back in his chair and placed his hands on the armrests, elbows out, and stared at the table.

She pushed a potato off her plate for the dog. She heard the long horn of a boat waiting for the Ballard Bridge to open and waited for the short horn that she knew must be coming.

"And what if we never use them?" he asked. "Do we bury them? Flush them? Is this all just a laboratory experiment?"

The wind shifted and the back door slammed shut. Kate lifted her head with a start and met Ben's eyes. She rested her elbows on the table and covered her closed eyelids with her fingertips. The dog walked toward the door.

"I guess gold is a dumb color," she said, putting her knife and fork together on her plate. "Eleven months of the year it's just another tree next to an ugly gold house."

He reached under his glasses with an index finger and rubbed his right eye. He sighed. "I mean maybe. If it's that important. If you can't live without them. I guess…"

She blew her nose into her white napkin and looked at her plate, avoiding his eyes. She brought the coffee pot to the table and filled his cup. He wasn't going anywhere.

"What do you say we skip the vegetables this year?" he said. "Maybe we should have flower beds, tulips, and daffodils and one of those wildflower seed packs. Maybe some strawberries. All flowers and strawberries. How does that sound? We could have ice cream. Ice cream and fresh berries every night for dinner all summer long. Wouldn't that be nice?"

Kate pulled her striped legs up to her chest and looked out the door at the robinia. Just last night, the dog had barked up into that tree. When she shined a flashlight on the branches, she saw two raccoons. She was surprised how untroubled they looked. Their stares were steady. They looked at each other and dug their nails into the trunk a little deeper. They didn't seem worried or in a rush to go anywhere. They seemed to know they were treed and that there was nothing they could do about it, it was just the way things were. Before she went back inside, she jiggled the flashlight back and forth, yelled and stomped her feet just to see if she could get a reaction. But the raccoons kept their gazes steady and continued to stare into the beam of her flashlight as simply as if it were the moon.

It Was Her Lemon Now

On Saturday night, Kate slipped on her navy sling backs and a knit dress to take her tumor and retracted nipple to her grandfather's ninetieth birthday party. Her parents reserved the corner room at his favorite restaurant, the one his architect friend designed back in the day. Kate passed the evening next to Ben, drinking sake and staring at the candle on their table, watching to see if it would be extinguished by the draft.

Later that night at home, Kate sat on the sofa next to her grandfather's prized lemon tree to read her biopsy report. She'd opened her new book on breast cancer and was learning about the abnormal cells in her ducts and lobes when Ben came down the stairs to ask if she was coming to bed.

"It's the highest histologic grade," she said. "I guess that means the cells are really fucked up."

"Doesn't seem like a good time to be doing this," he said, sitting in the leather chair.

"When would be?" she said. "Sleep is unlikely."

"How about a yogurt?" he asked. She usually ate a small bowl before bed. "Or tea. I'll make some tea."

Kate folded the biopsy report in half, put it in the book, and placed the book in the drawer of the coffee table. When the yogurt and tea were ready, she kissed Ben goodnight and took them downstairs to the basement. She stretched out on the couch with the dog at her side and turned on the television, flipping channels until she settled on a makeover show that dispensed the rules of fashion.

That night she learned that French cuffs were a good way to add flair, that brightly colored pieces could change her perspective, that charcoal gray business suits provided style and professionalism, that ponchos were bad, that shimmer powder could bring light to the eyes, that vertically lined trousers encouraged a long, lean look, and that what made her different, made her special.

On Monday morning Kate slipped on her Paris-washed, skinny-legged jeans and her red Mary Janes and went with Ben to wait in a tiny exam room with dust-colored furniture. Kate put on a flecked gown and the tissue paper crinkled as she sat on the exam table. The door opened, and in one fluid motion the fuzzy-haired surgeon handed Kate a binder, tapped the mouse on her desk, and started a tape recorder.

"Shows some skin involvement here." She pointed with her ballpoint at the crescent moon on the monitor. "Swelling. There's swelling."

Kate leaned forward. If she hadn't been wearing the gown, she would have moved closer but she didn't want her butt crack exposed—even if there was no one to see it. The floor looked cold. She should have left her socks on. Surely, the surgeon didn't need to examine her toes.

Ben squatted behind the doctor.

"Some swelling, edema," she continued, tilting her head. "Looks like there are tentacles reaching out from the primary tumor toward the chest wall. You'll need a mastectomy."

Kate sat up straight and wiped her hand over the binder and the words *From Discovery to Recovery.* She pictured her white, white skin, red blood, and a sharp blade, like a box cutter, leaving a red *O* on her chest where her breast used to be. *Sure,* Kate thought, *a mastectomy, of course.* Her C-cup breasts were relatively small compared to an egg-sized tumor with tentacles. *But the pain. God, it must hurt to have your breast cut off.*

Kate shifted her weight, unsticking her thighs where they spilled over the tissue.

"Will she need chemotherapy?" Ben asked.

"Probably," the doctor said, not looking away from the monitor. "There's also a spot of activity on the sternum."

"What's that mean, exactly? The spot. A tumor?" Ben asked.

"It may have spread to the bones. We'll need to do a full-body scan to find out for sure."

"A mastectomy," Kate said, wrapping her fingers around the top of the binder, holding it to her chest. "Really?"

The surgeon pulled out the table extension. Kate laid back. The doctor padded around on Kate's breasts with icy fingertips and held a magnifying glass to her skin. Kate noticed the red lipstick had bled into the creases around the doctor's mouth.

"Yes," she said. "Skin involvement. I'm sorry, but you have inflammatory breast cancer."

Kate sat up and reached around her neck, flicking the back of her gown closed. She'd read the first sentence of the chapter on inflammatory breast cancer that said it was the most aggressive form and skipped the rest, thinking, *Well, at least I don't have THAT.*

The doctor pointed to a laminated diagram of a woman's chest with a football-shaped dotted line where the breast used to be. Kate heard: tissue removal, drains, skin sparing, prophylactic.

"Must hurt," Kate said. "For a long time, right?"

The doctor stopped the recorder, handed the cassette to Ben, and told them the next scan appointment was Thursday. Results by Friday. Over Kate's head, a paper-mâché woman hung with her legs apart, suspended in mid-leap forever.

Kate wasn't a model or even much of a fashion plate, though she felt a bit more like one whenever she wore red shoes. She was a writer, a sailor, and an aspiring gardener who had strong bones and especially good plaque-reducing saliva. She wanted a baby boy named Theo after her grandfather. She wanted to finish her overdue article on the spring sailing championship. She wanted to find the right messenger-style handbag.

Instead of doing any of this after the doctor's appointment, Kate went home. She walked right in the front door, past the lemon tree, and through the French doors that led to the backyard. She crawled onto the grass between the lilacs and vegetables like she was climbing into bed. The sobs came from the lump on her sternum and escaped through her rectangular-shaped mouth. White skin. Red blood. Sharp blade. The turf was dry on top, but there was moisture down there somewhere, down where the grubs and worms lived. She dug her fingertips into the grass. There was something real about the smell of damp soil, and she knew when she found it, it would be unchanged.

Kate rolled over and the brown hair she would soon be without fell across her face. She heard a gate unlatch, the click of a leash onto a dog's collar, and the high-pitched hum of her neighbor, Phyllis. Kate pulled her knees under her body and stood and as soon as Phyllis' orange-gray bun disappeared down the alley, she went inside.

Kate curled up on the couch and retrieved the big book from the drawer. Ben stepped through the front door with his laptop backpack hanging from his shoulder.

"It's not a question of if it comes back," Kate said without looking up. "With inflammatory breast cancer, it's a question of when."

He sat on the ottoman. "I'm sure that's out of date," he said, dropping his shoulders and putting his keys on the coffee table.

"I can't wait another week," she said.

There were plants Kate gauged her life by—the lady slippers in the forest, the lilacs she and Ben had planted their first spring in the house—plants whose successes seemed to be the key to her own. Plants whose blossoms or deaths became her proudest moments or personal failures.

Kate's grandfather's lemon tree was one of these plants. It had been unhappy in his dark apartment, and Ben, eager to please the old man, had volunteered a home for the botanical diva. She still thought of it as her grandfather's tree, but it was in her home. It was her lemon now.

When it first came to live with them last fall, Kate placed the glazed green pot and waxy oval-shaped leaves next to the southwest-facing windows. It sprouted bright new growth from its upper branches. She thought it would be happy there and used to find comfort sitting in the leather chair next to its corner.

But that evening, Kate found no comfort. She stayed on the couch until midnight. Ben came downstairs in the white bathrobe she'd bought for his birthday. He'd said it was the worst gift he'd ever been given. She liked soft things like cashmere socks, silk pajamas, and long scarves that wrapped twice around her neck, but he liked gifts that needed power. She knew that now, and that he liked mustard on both pieces of sandwich bread, mochas with half the chocolate, and cherry, but not apple, pie.

No, she said, couldn't sleep. No, she wasn't planning on going to bed. Ben picked up his book, stretched out on the couch, and wiped his eyes under his glasses. Kate climbed over his body and pressed her head into the curve of his neck.

"Why do you have to go there?" he asked. "Why can't you just assume you will be the one that makes it?"

"Tell me a story," she said. "Any story."

Ben told her their story. A young couple in a neighborhood tavern. She dropped off a friend. Didn't intend to stay. He asked her to play pool. She said U2 was a bore and selected Beastie Boys from the juke box. The man in the orange track suit asked her to dance. A stained-glass window broke, letting the moonlight shine on their feet. Another day, they went sailing. He was driving. The boom crashed back and forth over their heads. She knew the main was too tight and let it out. He knew they would sail together again. Later in the warm bar she wrapped her hands around a hot chocolate while he drank coffee, dark rum, and lime juice. When he walked her to her door, he told her that time stopped when they met but meant that his watch needed a new battery. His lips had tasted like key-lime pie.

Eventually his steady breathing became a raspy snore. Kate listened to his heart, making an impression on his chest while he slept. She'd always hoped and even assumed that they'd be married for fifty years or more. She looked out the window and watched the stars cluster around the moon like a cobweb, but she was uncomfortable being so close to the lemon so late at night. A few weeks after they got the plant, leaf holes appeared. Her grandpa said they were from slugs that must have nested in the dirt when it lived outside his apartment. They hid in the daytime and came out to eat at night. She imagined them slithering over the rim of the pot, over her leather chair, high-fiving each other as they spun in their slow, slimy way around her living room. She left the living room to the slugs at night because she'd heard that once they'd gotten into the soil there wasn't much anyone could do.

She lifted her body from Ben's. It was time to watch that make-over show with all the fashion rules. She'd always been one to follow the rules and at first, it seemed impossible that she had cancer, but after living with it for a week it would have seemed impossible if she did not.

That night Kate learned to not ever wear berets, even if it matched her jacket, especially if it matched her jacket; that good wrap dresses emphasized the waist; that the key to a "five-minute face" was shimmering highlight underneath the eyebrow, on the inside corner of the eye, and on the top of the cheekbone; that pointy shoes lengthened the leg; that plastic clothes were bad; that cuts were more important than patterns; that bustier collections never worked; that every woman should own a suit; that metallic sneakers existed for people of all ages; to wear only one snazzy item at a time to keep from looking like a clown; to choose longer hemlines for more elegant and mature looks; to pair bold patterns and colors with neutrals; and to never wear glittery clogs or glue shells to fabric.

By the time test day finally arrived Kate felt like the plywood crow perched on Phyllis' railing—she was a silhouette of herself. She pulled on her old Levi's, a stretched-out waffle knit top, and clogs with her old hiking socks.

In a dark, windowless, drafty room a nurse hooked up her IV and brought her a thin, pilled blanket that barely covered her legs. With gloved hands he unscrewed the top of a stainless steel canister that looked like a nuclear weapon. When he leaned over her chair to inject the radioactive substance into her veins, she saw the bald spots in his goatee at the corners of his mouth that he attempted to hide with a moustache comb-over.

When the scan was over, Kate explained to a technician, who needed a little shimmer powder around her eyes, that she had a spot on her sternum and that she'd been waiting for so long already. Kate begged her to find a pathologist to give her some preliminary results.

"I need to know," she said. "I need to know if I'm dying."

"Sorry," the technician said. "Nothing I can do."

At home, Kate watered the lemon. A few weeks ago, she'd noticed dense, dark cobwebs—tight like cotton fuzz or dog tail fur—tangled in the branches. Her grandfather instructed her to spray with insecticidal soap, and she did. Then she lifted the pot onto a pedestal so its branches were eye level with the windows. But the lemon was weak and depressed, out of its climate of eternal sunshine, and she realized it had to fight its own battle against the microscopic, web-making, eight-legged bastards. It had the best spot in the house, but she knew that even with the best care and the sunniest, warmest corner, a lemon could die.

It wasn't dark yet, the time she usually watched TV, but she didn't know what else to do. That makeover show was always playing on some channel somewhere. Say no to tube socks. Navels are never appropriate in the classroom. Don't take dressing cues from Dad. Don't wear pigtails. Hide a tummy with a fitted jacket. Heels can be comfortable. Don't wear crappy children's shirts unless you're a crappy child. Wide-leg trouser jeans in dark washes are invaluable. Emphasize the top half to even out a heavy bottom half. Cute is good when you're five. Every woman should have at least one outfit for a sophisticated evening out. Tuxedo pants are flattering to the leg, especially when worn with great heels. A shirt should come over the top of the pant. Create balanced silhouettes. Don't be afraid of shoes.

Kate opened the binder from the surgeon's office. Maybe it would tell her what it meant to have cancer in the bones. Would she need a bone marrow transplant? Would she live in a bubble? Or would they treat her at all? Maybe they would tell her that she only had weeks to live. A breast was one thing. A breast could be taken off, its absence hidden with a prosthetic and a good wrap dress. But bones. Bones were the structure of the body, the foundation, the formation, the straight-leg pant.

The dog walked across the floor upstairs and she considered calling Ben, her mom, her friend Tami. But she needed someone who had this, this cancer in the bones thing, to tell her what happened next. Inside the front pocket of the binder was a pink brochure that said *Angel Network*. They made six contacts with every new patient and made sure they all got enough hugs.

It wasn't really a hotline but it sounded like they all had cancer. She didn't want to cry, but by the time the woman answered, she was.

Kate told the hug-giver that the doctors thought it was in her bones and she was waiting for the results and wanted to hear from someone who had this. Was there anyone there, at this Angel Network, who had it in their bones?

The line was quiet. "No," she said.

"Then what?" Kate said. "They're all dead, aren't they? Then what? What have you got? Anything, just tell me. Tell me what happened to you."

Teresa said the first time she was diagnosed she had a lumpectomy and eighteen of her twenty lymph nodes tested positive for cancer. She found another tumor in the same breast a year later.

This was bad, Kate knew that. But bones were beyond nodes. Even worse. Unspeakable. Kate pulled up her legs on the couch and sobbed. She tried to speak, to say anything, but snot and tears ran down her face without a Kleenex in sight. She ran her fleece-covered forearm under her nose.

"What happens then?" It sounded more like, *whahabensden.* "If, the bones, I mean. Do doctors treat it? Or do I just wait to die?"

"I'm no doctor but I do know women who have cancer in their bones and they do treat it."

"Can I talk to one? Talk to one of these women with the bone thing?"

"We don't have one here now."

"How will I? I can't..."

"Do you have faith or spiritual beliefs?"

"No."

"Have you joined a support group?"

"I'm only thirty-one. All the support groups are for women like my mom."

But Teresa knew a group for young women, and Kate—breathing again but tired, thirsty, wet—took down the name, hung up the phone, and turned on the television.

Great skin is the secret to true beauty. Microderm abrasion scrapes away dead layers of the skin, making it smooth and less red. Banded seams that stretch around the waist, hold you in and narrow the top of the hip. Princess Leia hair knobs are never a good idea. Sleeves should not come down to your knuckles. It takes practice to walk in a good heel. You can lose twenty-five pounds by changing your clothes. You can do good and love yourself.

The doctor promised to call by one o'clock on Friday.

Oral hygiene is important. You have to be eighty to wear Christmas sweaters. Shoulder pads are ridiculous. Skirts should not be covered in pineapples. Some style is good.

Two o'clock passed.

Wearing mommy jeans is a cry for help. V-necks elongate. When mixing prints, be sure one is dominant and the other is supporting.

Then three o'clock. Perhaps it had spread so far that they had to consult an expert.

Skirts that float away from the body make the waist look smaller.

They'd probably never seen anything like it. Didn't know how she'd lived so long.

Focused highlights through the top of the hair give lift and brightness. An illusion neckline brings attention to the face. Skirts that have volume de-emphasize the mid-section. Empire waists elongate. It's all worth it.

Probably would only live a few more days. At four o'clock she left the surgeon a message. The phone rang and she pressed the mute button on the remote.

"Activity only in your left breast," the surgeon said.

"Only?"

"Sternum lump didn't light up."

"Not cancer?"

"Doesn't appear to be."

After calling Ben, Kate sat on the wet deck, next to the lemon tree Ben had just moved outside. She wrapped her arms around her waist and rested her forehead on her bent knees. Her heart valves opened and closed and she felt the blood move into her toes. Phyllis walked by wearing white pumps that clicked in rhythm with her humming, red cotton socks folded down, cotton pants covered with vines and flowers that were not loose or tight and hit just above the ankle, an electric blue turtleneck with stretched-out sleeves, and a seventies' style knee-length fur and leather coat that was draped over her shoulders like a cape. She looked beautiful.

The lemon smelled citrus sweet and the soil damp. Kate pulled the tiny paintbrush from the dirt and brushed the pistils and stamens of the two new white blossoms to help the lemon pollinate. When she finished, she lay back on the wet deck, letting the water soak through her T-shirt, and stretched her arms over her head. She dreamed of glittery clogs, crappy children's T-shirts, and skinny-leg jeans. When Kate opened her eyes, she stared at the lemon's leaves in the sunshine and noticed they looked greener, the same way grass looked greener when set against a clear blue sky.

Who in This Room

When your doctor says *invasive carcinoma,* you will cry, right there in her office. She says you need twenty-seven weekly chemotherapy treatments, a mastectomy, radiation, and five years of hormone-blocking drugs. You will be thinking of chemotherapy, picturing yourself passed out on the cold tile bathroom floor, and wondering if you will see your thirty-second birthday.

At your first chemotherapy appointment you will sit in a green vinyl recliner while a nurse looks for a vein in your hand. She will draw a blood sample. You will swallow three small pills, but the anti-nausea medications won't help your nervous stomach. Before the nurse leaves the room, she will tell you to watch the video about what to expect from chemotherapy, running in a continuous loop on channel eighteen. It will tell you to eat if you are hungry and sleep if you are tired. It will tell you to talk to your spouse about how you are feeling. Later, at home, you will tell your husband the thought of washing the dishes makes you feel nauseous. It will be true.

The nurse will return with a vial filled with something that looks like cherry-flavored cough syrup. She will ask your name and birth date. You will watch the life-saving poison enter the vein in your hand. Twenty minutes later when you go to the bathroom your urine will be pink. You will begin to hate pink.

When you get home, you will think you are going to vomit. Carry the big yellow bowl around the house. You will vomit.

The next morning, and every morning except Tuesdays and Wednesdays, just before he leaves for work, your husband will wake you up for a shot intended to boost your dangerously low white blood cell count. While his hands shake, you will whisper, "Just do it, just do it fast." You will do this every day. Even on your birthday. Even on your anniversary.

He will start calling himself Dr. B.

One weekend morning he will be out of town and you will try to give yourself the shot. Carefully loading the syringe, you will sit with the needle poised over your abdomen for twenty minutes, unable to inflict more pain on yourself, until you will be late for coffee with your sister. Bring the loaded syringe to the Starbucks and, in the bathroom, tell your sister to overcome her fear of needles and do what you cannot do for yourself. Tell her to "Just do it fast." Call her Dr. E.

Your mouth will taste like you've been sucking on a paper clip. Rinse with cinnamon-flavored mouthwash.

You will read all six hundred pages of *The Breast Book* and know your nuclear grade, Her2 status, and Bloom-Richardson score. You will go online to find survival statistics for women with your type of cancer. Really, you will be looking for someone to tell you that you are going to be okay. When you discover your chance of surviving five years is less than ten percent, you will stop searching. You will stop reading. Your left eyelid will twitch for three days.

A small disk with a tube running directly into the blood vessel near your collarbone will be surgically implanted under your skin so the nurses can administer chemotherapy without using the vein in your hand. The disk will stick out of your chest like an alien baby. You will call it Bobby. Your husband will ask the doctor if it plays MP3s.

A friend will send you a gift basket with a pink teddy bear, pink socks, and a pink nail file. Send her a thank you note even though you hate pink.

Three weeks after your first chemotherapy, your pubic hair will fall out. Your head hair will go next, then your brows, lashes, and nose hair.

You will cover your baldness with a dark green scarf that matches your eyes. Tie the ends in the back like a bun.

When your mother sees you, she will cry. She will buy you an expensive handbag because it makes you both feel better. You will call it the cancer bag. Later, you will buy cancer shoes, cancer earrings, and eventually a cancer car.

You and your husband will go away for the weekend. Lying in bed you will feel the poison in your veins and wonder if it is working. Try to visualize the tumor dissolving like Alka-Seltzer in water.

You will look at the ceiling and think about the twenty remaining treatments. You will cry. You will think about the children you never had. You will think about leaving your husband a young, childless widower. Go home early and rent a movie starring Reese Witherspoon.

You will become constipated and bleed into the toilet. You will go online and post a message about your bowel problems on a breast cancer bulletin board. Take 900 mg of magnesium a day.

A friend will have a hat and scarf party and serve your favorite foods, which by then will be Tater Tots and catsup. You will drink seltzer water without ice, and they will tell you that you have a beautifully shaped head because they don't know what else to say. You will wonder what you used to talk about.

You will read a memoir written by a twenty-seven-year-old breast cancer survivor. Really, you will be looking for a friend who knows what it's like, but when you learn that she had seventeen bridesmaids in her wedding, you will realize you have nothing in common. Go online and find a local support group.

At home you will stare out the window and miss your old life. You will realize that bad things do happen and you start thinking about all the other bad things that could happen. You will spend two days in your pajamas.

You will stop sleeping. The dog will lick the back of your bald head while you lie on the couch. Take him for a walk along your usual route, passing close to the duck pond so you can feel the familiar tug of his leash, taking the tunnel under the train tracks to the boulders where the beach changes from rocks to sand.

You will be relieved when the northerly picks up as it usually does on sunny afternoons and you will scan the water, looking for the seal that slaps his fin on the surface. When he does not appear, you will think that he may be gone forever.

You will go to the bathroom five times every night. Buy a night-light.

You will decide the chemotherapy isn't working. You will spend your thirty-second birthday trying to convince yourself you aren't about to die.

You will begin to look forward to your surgery. Remind yourself that breasts are not a vital organ, not crucial to your survival. Try to convince yourself you never really liked that breast anyway.

You will celebrate your third wedding anniversary with a four-hour visit to the oncology ward for your tenth chemotherapy.

You will make an appointment to see a therapist who will tell you that everything you are feeling is normal. You will tell her you are obsessed with death. She will tell you to make a list of positive affirmations. Even though you think it's corny, make the list and carry it in your pocket.

Your husband will start wearing a pink bracelet—which he will call a "men's sport band"—even though you both hate pink.

Your hot flashes will start with bulging veins in your hands, then travel up your arms to your chest. Your heart will race. You will reach for a drink of water—your body anticipating the fluid you are about to lose—and your cheeks will burn red as you tear off your scarf and shirt. Sweat will dribble down the sides of your bald head. Try not to remove your clothes in public.

Go ahead and make "hotflash" a verb and use it as a landmark for activities in your day. For example, "I was hotflashing in my therapist's office when…"

Your eyes will feel like dry rocks in their sockets because even your tears have stopped working. They no longer lubricate. Don't bother with drops, they won't work.

After you fill your prescription for sleeping pills, you will dream that spiders are crawling down your arms into your mouth and killing you from the inside. You will scream in the darkness until your husband turns on the light.

The next day you will see a naturopath who will look at your tongue and ask how your dreams have been. You will tell him about the spiders. He will ask what you think is causing the bad dreams. You will decide he is an idiot, but that won't stop you from buying $295 worth of vitamins in the hope that they will keep your fingernails from falling off.

You will realize you are halfway though chemotherapy and be both happy and depressed.

By now you will have stopped throwing up as often, but you will still feel nauseous. You will stop eating and start losing weight.

Someone will suggest marijuana and you will think this is a very good idea. You will task your husband with the acquisition. He will go to the Gob Shop on his lunch break and buy his favorite tools.

A green pipe. A yellow bong you will name Sunshine. His bowling buddy will sell him his personal stash. In the basement of your house, your husband will teach you to smoke. You will cough into the bong and shoot a stream of water over the coffee table and onto the dog. You won't feel any different.

As an aspiring drug user you will spend your days in the basement alternating between hilarious sportfishing and hilarious makeover shows. Bake scones and eat five in a row.

Play the country western music your sister put on your iPod. Sing "Don't It Make My Brown Eyes Blue" to your brown-eyed dog. You will think this is very funny.

When your husband comes home from work, you will want him to tell you about every moment of his day, but when he speaks, his words will evaporate into the air like smoke. Just enjoy watching his lips move. Tell him you've been practicing very hard, but your pot smoking just doesn't seem to be working.

You will buy a jigsaw puzzle and decide it is too hard. It will sit on a table in your basement for six months.

When your mother-in-law comes to visit, talk to her casually about the pot-smoking skills you are cultivating. Then ask her what she would like for dinner. Over a cup of tea, tell her about the rest of your treatment. Tell her your tumor is hormone-receptor-positive and that it needs estrogen to grow and that after radiation you will be on hormone-blocking drugs for at least five years. Tell her that even if you do come out of medical menopause, you are not allowed to get pregnant while on these drugs. Tell her that her youngest son won't be having any biological children.

Friends will visit. They will bring soup. Your baldness will frighten their children. They will cry. You will cry.

You will switch chemo drugs. Before your first treatment, the nurse will give you steroids to prevent an allergic reaction. Your husband will make a joke about your batting average and the nurse will roll her eyes. This chemo will smell different and burn the inside of your nose like alcohol. Your husband will tell you this chemo comes from the yew tree. You won't care.

　　At home you will feel great and buzz around the house. You will eat. Yogurt, bananas, Tater Tots, scones. You will clean the toilet. You will eat again. You will do the dishes. The next day you will be exhausted. Next week the nurse will tell you it was the steroids.

You will celebrate being nausea-free. Take a trip to visit your sister in San Francisco. Listen to live music, eat nachos, buy a new jacket, and forget, for a moment, that you are bald.

You will run out of pot. Don't get more.

You will have diarrhea and won't make it to the bathroom in time. Sip Imodium straight from the bottle. Don't use the pills—they are too strong—just keep sipping until your bowels are under control. Buy a small bottle to carry in the cancer bag.

You will tell your therapist you are still obsessed with death. She will say death is a landscape that you can visit, but you can't stay. You will realize you've constructed a semi-permanent yurt in your landscape and it may be time to pack up and move on.

Your nose will drip unexpectedly when you're talking to a friend. It will run all over the front of your shirt before you can catch it.

One Sunday night you will sit on the couch reading a book. You will feel okay. Notice that you feel okay and be grateful.

The smell of your oncologist's office will make your mouth water, like you need to vomit. Your body knows what is going on. Your mind tells it to stay. Every week you go back to the green vinyl recliner it is more difficult to stay, but you do stay and let them give you more poison. You tell yourself you will be okay.

Your yoga instructor will tell you to tell your body it is healing. Your body will call her a liar. Your body will be right.

Your red and white blood cell counts will get very low. Your husband will enter the last twenty weeks of data from your blood work into a spreadsheet and create pages of charts and graphs. You will become obsessed with your cellular activity and uncovering the cause of fluctuations in your Absolute Neutrophil Count (ANC). When your numbers are up, you will wonder if it was a result of the orange you ate, the vitamin you took, the sunshine you sat in.

When you express concern over your skyrocketing Alanine Aminotransferase (ALS), which could signify liver damage, your doctor will say, "Who in this room has been to medical school?" You will decide you hate her.

You will become more and more confused. First you will forget words, like *saucer*, then conversations, then friends. You will go to the gas station. It will take you three tries to get your gas tank positioned next to the pump.

Your fingers and toes will feel prickly, like they're asleep when they're not. Take 15 mg of L-Glutamine twice a day with yogurt.

You can stop carrying your list of positive affirmations because you will have it memorized. Write your favorite poem on a small scrap of paper and carry it in your pocket. Repeat it to yourself. Memorize it.

Because your last treatment is scheduled during the week before Christmas, you will start preparing for the holidays in October. You will say "Merry Christmas" to trick-or-treaters and dress up as a Christmas tree for a Halloween party. You will win a prize for best costume because the hostess feels sorry for you.

You will develop uncharacteristic punctuality problems.

Before Thanksgiving, your husband will buy you a small snow globe from the grocery store. You will bring it with you to chemotherapy. Your college friend will bring pumpkin bread and stories of her New Zealand honeymoon to your appointment. She will bump the snow globe, and it will fall from the table and break. You will yell "Christmas is ruined!" and laugh.

You will bring Gatorade bottles full of used syringes from your daily shots to deposit in the Sharps container at your doctor's office. You will chat with your favorite nurse about her trip to the Philippines and her boyfriend who still lives there. You will ask the receptionist about her weekend barbeque. You will swing by the pharmacy for your prescriptions. You will talk with the parking attendant about the crazy weather. You will wish this wasn't your routine and that you didn't have so many friends in the oncology ward.

You will look at yourself in the mirror and see skin the color of dry cement. You will ask your husband to take photos of you without your scarf, with your red eyes and bald head. You will want these photos. You won't know why.

Your hips will hurt. You will limp and have a hard time standing straight. You will get winded walking the dog. When you go to the beach to sit on the driftless driftwood, you will forget to look for the seal but notice the common loon and the pink bill of the black oystercatchers and wonder if they've been there all along.

When you have three treatments left, your nails will pull away from their fingers. You will forget to buy more multi-vitamins and get a head cold that will turn into a sinus infection. When you sneeze, your nose will bleed. Your white blood cell count will get so low that you will be afraid your doctor won't give you your last treatment. You won't be afraid of the neutropenic fever, infection, and/or hospitalization that may result if she does.

Two nights before your last treatment, you will stub your toe on the coffee table. Because your platelet count is low, it will turn your foot blue. You will limp in to your last chemo with a sinus infection, bloody nose, and broken toe. You will be sure your white blood cell count will be too low to get your last chemo. There will be no flowers or balloons. You will want to be done even if it kills you. When your doctor finally approves the order, you won't have anything left for celebration.

Instead of cheering you will lean back in the green vinyl recliner and turn your head away from the IV. You will realize your breath sounds like a snore, and your mouth is hanging open, and that you must be doing something like sleeping.

You will wait for the bag to drain and know only that there will be more waiting. Waiting for the MRI. Waiting for the results. Waiting for surgery. Waiting for the results. Waiting for radiation. Waiting for hormone-blocking drugs. You will wait and hope that someday all this waiting will end.

Remember to swing by your doctor's office to thank her for saving your life.

You will calculate that in six months you received 154 shots, ingested 210 chemotherapy pills and 240 anti-nausea pills, took 60 sleeping pills, and spent 140 hours sitting in a green vinyl recliner in the oncology ward receiving 27 chemotherapy treatments for a total of nearly two gallons of intravenous medicine/poison—some of it from the yew tree. You will be surprised you are alive.

At home your husband will give you a small box. Inside will be a pair of diamond earrings. You like shiny things and they will make you smile.

A friend will give you a gift basket with pink candies, pink playing cards, and a pink teddy bear. You already have a pink teddy bear. Call the dog into the kitchen where you are sorting through the basket. Squat down to his level and breathe in his sweet fishy breath. Notice the tartar build-up on his brown teeth and his sharp incisors as you place the bear in his mouth. Watch his jaws compress the horrific pinkness. Let him out into the December rain and watch him paw the bear into the mud, secure that it is safely outside your home, even if it's only for today.

Here's the Secret

When Kate met Julie in their shared oncologists' office, Julie's goal had been to live to her thirtieth birthday. Kate was new to cancer, but Julie was a veteran, just diagnosed with her recurrence. She told Kate which nurses were nice, where to buy cute scarves, and which brow pencils worked best.

It wasn't long before Julie's kidneys started to fail and Kate helped organize a group of cancer-survivor friends to bring her meals and take her to doctor's appointments. Julie named the group after her favorite flower. She called them her "Tulips."

A hot spring day, a year and a half after they met, Kate climbed the steps of her house with a bag of groceries, the ingredients for the last dish Kate would ever make for Julie—the dish she would take to Julie's service. As Kate opened her front door, she saw a youngish man with low-slung jeans ring her neighbor's bell.

He came for Kate next, and when he rang, she could see him and he could see her through the stained-glass window on her door. There was no use hiding. She would open the door to tell him she wasn't interested in whatever he was selling.

"I really like what you've done here," he gestured with a limp hand at the tulip-lined bed near the front door. He was cultivating the look of a teenager, a skateboard slipped under his arm, but his voice had a depth and rasp that came from age and years of smoking.

Kate could tell by the way he flicked his wrist but watched her face that he didn't give a shit about her flowers, but his compliment caught her off-guard.

A few months before Julie died, Kate, in her duty as a flower, took her to a radiation appointment. As Kate pulled into the driveway, Julie was saying good-bye to her four-year-old daughter, Lauren. Julie introduced Kate to the girl who sat in her car seat with her arms crossed. "Give me a kiss," Julie said. "Now leave me with a smile."

Once on the road, Julie said the pain was worse. She had called her oncologist.

"This isn't good," Julie shook her head. "I guess it was bad yesterday too but I wouldn't admit it. Today there's no denying it." She sighed and refastened the clip in her short blonde hair.

They parked close to the door and sat next to a window in the waiting area. Julie told Kate about the Cherokee medicine man who had traveled from Montana to Seattle to save her. "He's one of the few who work on white people." She arched her back in her chair. "Erik's uncle knows him. He's super busy and stuff. He came as a personal favor." She ran her hand along her flat chest and the top of her distended abdomen. "I can't tell you exactly what happened, but I can tell you he said the pain would get worse before it got better. And this is different today. It's higher. Could it work this quick?"

"Doesn't hurt to hope," Kate said, placing her hand on Julie's.

When the nurse called her name, Julie stood up, belly first, and moved slowly down the hall, arms bent around her torso. In the examination room the nurse said Julie had a fever.

"That explains why I dressed Lauren in shorts," Julie said, leaning back on the exam table with her knees bent. The white stripe of her sweat pants hung over her slip-on tennis shoes.

The nurse said Julie had gained four pounds in two days.

The oncologist said he'd called a surgical consult.

"No," Julie said looking at Kate. "Diane went into surgery and Diane never woke up."

"No one's suggested surgery yet," Kate said, patting Julie's knee with a flat hand.

"What can I do for you?" Kate asked the man. She'd forgotten her plan to tell him she wasn't interested, but she remembered she needed to prepare the dish and get in the shower so her curly hair would have time to air-dry before she had to leave.

"I'm trying to raise $10,000," he said. "So I can go to my high school's public speaking camp in Boston." He dropped his head to look at the ground, and Kate noticed the pock marks on his cheekbones and the gray hair at his temples. This man wasn't a boy, and probably wasn't a student.

After radiation, Julie told Kate that just last week, she'd been thinking she had her thirtieth birthday in the bag. It was only six weeks away and she'd been feeling good.

When the surgeon arrived and placed his hand on her abdomen, Julie yelled, slapped it away, then apologized twice.

The doctor stepped back from the exam table, crossed his arms, and stood with his legs wide. "Well, as you know," he said, "you have a huge inoperable tumor in your abdomen..."

Julie squeaked, moved her fingers to her lips, and then covered her wet eyes. "No one's ever used the word 'huge' before," she said.

The surgeon apologized and said this was just the kind of guy he was. He told it straight, like he saw it. Not one to sugar-coat. He said they needed another CT to know what was happening now, and that he'd have to admit her to the hospital to get her pain under control.

Julie was on the phone to her husband, Erik, before the door had clicked shut. After Erik, she called a Tulip and asked her to pick up Lauren from preschool and let her make a mini-pizza for dinner. Erik arrived and Julie was chatting with the nurses when Kate kissed her good-bye. She drove straight to a mall where she wandered for three hours before she eventually bought some bedding that was too expensive, even on sale.

Kate didn't have time for this. She sighed and was turning away when the clatter of his skateboard hitting her walkway startled her.

"I've been working on my tricks. Watch this." Beads of sweat gathered next to the gray hairs. He jumped in the air and the board rose with him, flipping under his feet. Kate remembered a college friend who was always practicing that move—an ollie or a kickflip or something like that. The board came back down, landing on its wheels and his feet soon followed, but his left foot hit the edge of the board and flipped it onto its side. He twisted his ankle and his hands reached the ground just before his hip.

Kate cringed.

"Fuck," he said under his breath, regaining his balance. Kate asked if he was okay. "Damn," he said, noticing the axle had broken free. "I special goddamn ordered this shit. Special goddamn ordered."

Julie's CT results showed the already "huge" tumor had doubled in size and was pushing vital organs out of its way. Her doctor didn't want to give a prognosis, but when pressed, he said she had a month, tops. Two days later, Julie went home, covered in a quilt of pain patches and under hospice care.

Chaos engulfed the flower world when word spread that Julie had a month to live. She was flooded with emails, phone calls, and cards. From her bed at home, Julie posted a message on her blog that said: *For god's sake, I'm not dead yet!*

The man-boy rubbed his ankle. "I got these friends." His tone had changed. It was cold, hard and he spoke deliberately. "They're not like me. They don't got no goals. They're kind of night owls. They like to hang around your neighborhood. At night." He emphasized "night" both times.

Oh, Kate thought with a sharp intake of breath. Now she knew what this was about.

"They call themselves street artists," he squinted a bit, concentrating his menace. "You know what that is?"

"Graffiti?" Kate said. She pictured him wandering her neighborhood at night, slouching under a hooded sweatshirt with his hands in his front pocket.

Two weeks after the prognosis, Kate found herself on Julie's front porch with ten other Tulips. She was carrying a goopy casserole that she felt bad about bringing after Julie told her she hadn't eaten since Wednesday, when her doctor discovered a bowel obstruction.

"I'm really not hungry," Julie said from the hospital bed in their bedroom. "It's been almost a week and I'm not hungry at all. I just wish..." Julie stared at the ceiling. "I just wish I'd known my last meal would be my last meal, you know? I didn't eat much that day and finally my sister-in-law talked me into a peanut butter and jelly sandwich. That was it, PB&J."

"Furthermore..." Julie glanced over her shoulder at the closed door and leaned toward the group. "It wasn't even that good," she whispered. "Too much peanut butter." She fell back onto her pillow with a smile. "But I do think I'm going to talk to my hospice nurse about alternate forms of nutrition. Starvation seems like a stupid way to die."

Everyone nodded. Yes—stupid—they agreed.

Lauren opened the door and jumped onto the bed. Her smile exposed a tiny dimpled chin just like her father's. She showed the Tulips that her blue dress was reversible with orange on the other side.

"Okay, Honey," Julie said, talking into the top of Lauren's head. "Mommy needs some alone time with her friends." When Lauren did not move, Julie asked if she remembered what they talked about that morning—obeying the first time she was asked. The girl rolled off the far side of the bed and walked around the end. When she got to Kate, she climbed into her lap. Julie gave her a look and she dropped back to the floor and left the room.

One of the Tulips handed Julie a gift, a framed poem. Julie asked her to read it aloud. The Tulip's voice cracked when she got to the part about being changed forever by her friendship. When she finished, she handed the frame back to Julie.

"It would be nice if you read this at my transition," Julie said, looking at the words and running her fingers along the carved frame. "I'm calling it a celebration and transition. I've been working on

the arrangements this week. I don't want it to be a somber affair."
She looked up at Kate who sat at the foot of the bed. "Sad is okay, I
don't think it can be avoided, but not somber. Don't wear black. And
there won't be an open casket. Open caskets really creep me out." She
crinkled her nose.

"How are you doing?" Kate asked, pulling a tissue from the box
sitting on the bed. She knew Julie struggled with the existence of
God. "How are you doing spiritually?"

"When my friend Suzie died, she said, 'I know where I'm going
and I'm not afraid.'" Julie set the frame on her pillow. "I'm not religious like she was, but I can safely say I'm not afraid. I don't know
where I'm going, but I'm not afraid."

The room was quiet. One Tulip blew her nose.

Julie reached down next to her bed and brought up a box covered
in green and pink ribbon that was full of cards for Erik and Lauren
to receive at important future occasions—birthdays, anniversaries,
graduations, weddings. She included a picture and a note in each
one. She had to get back to it. That meant it was time for the Tulips
to go. Kate was the last to leave and when she did, she wondered at
what age Lauren would stop getting cards.

Kate stared over his head at the blue sky. She considered her flight.
She could turn, but she couldn't outrun him. He knew where she
lived.

"You're going to help me out," he said. It wasn't a question.

Kate wondered if he was the one who had dumped the stolen
Dodge in front of their house. Or the one who stole Ben's CDs from
his car. He probably traveled the country doing this. He'd case a
neighborhood during the day and return to burglarize in the night.

His goal had nothing to do with speaking and everything to do with her laptop, stereo, and diamond earrings.

Julie thought she'd never have another piece of birthday cake. Then, two weeks later, a scan showed the tumor near her liver had grown, but that the bowel obstruction was gone. "Highly unusual," her doctor said. "A miracle," her mother said. Julie started eating soft foods and planning her birthday, which was now only a week away.

When Kate and Ben arrived at the luau-themed party, Kate noticed the parchment-yellow of Julie's cheeks and the grayness around her eyes. Julie sat in the corner of a sectional with a shoulder bag filled with IV pain medication. When it was Kate's turn, she left Ben to talk with a Tulip and sat down next to Julie. Lauren climbed between them. She held a paper plate with just the pineapple picked off a piece of upside-down cake.

"That's my next goal," Julie said, "to walk Lauren to her first day of kindergarten." Julie smiled, but looked away. "I wish it didn't have to be this way," Julie said, wrapping her arm around the top of Lauren's head. "I wish I was going to be here every night to tuck Lauren into bed and blow sweet dreams into her ear." When Lauren looked up, Kate wiped a tear away with the knuckle of her thumb.

Lauren put her plate on the table, turned, and set her sticky hand on top of Kate's. "I know you're feeling sad," she said, "but Mommy will always be with us, in our hearts." She put a hand on her chest. Then she raised her arms and rocked side to side while singing a song. The tune was "Twinkle, Twinkle," but the words were about Julie being the best mommy and always being in her heart.

Lauren finished and both women told her the song was beautiful before Lauren ran out the door to jump on the trampoline. Julie said that the grief counselor had done great things for them.

When it was time to leave, Kate watched Julie give each guest a hug. Kate couldn't believe it was over so soon. It seemed like it had just started, that they had just met. Kate told herself Julie wasn't going anywhere. Her lips were still pink, her teeth white, and her eyes still velvet brown. When Julie pulled Kate close, she whispered, "You're doing all the right things."

Kate wanted to believe her.

The man stared at Kate. No one spoke.

"How can I help?" Kate asked.

He stepped on the good end of his board, flipped the broken end up, grabbed it with one hand, and reached into the back pocket of his jeans with the other. He handed Kate a brochure.

"I'm selling magazines today," he said flatly. "You just pick what you want and I'll tell you what it costs."

Kate wondered why he continued to pretend this was a fundraiser, why he didn't just demand the money, why they had to pretend this was fair, acceptable in any way, or anything other than it was. "Okay," Kate pointed to the first magazine that sounded interesting. "How about *National Geographic Traveler?*"

"Good choice," he said, pulling another pamphlet from his pocket. "That's fifty dollars cash, credit, or check."

Two weeks after her birthday, Julie dictated a message for Erik to post. *Do you want to know a secret? I was going to write a post about having a hard time today but that I knew tomorrow was a new day. It would have been the kind of message that made you think, 'Gee, that Julie sure is inspiring, nothing gets her down.' But then (here's the secret) I decided that was all bullshit.*

The tumor is continuing to push everything out of the way, causing more pain and the appearance that I am three months pregnant. The most disappointing part is that the only treatment is bed rest (I'm most comfortable when I'm perfectly still) and more pain meds. The problem with this? I don't want to be a bedridden vegetable. I had a crappy day today. Now this is the truth: it was bad. I mean real bad.

Good night, my dear Tulips.

One week later, Erik posted a message that Julie died peacefully.

Kate was afraid of identity theft. She didn't want to give him her credit card number or a check. But she only had $20 in her wallet. She went upstairs to where Ben was napping and found $5 in his wallet. She started counting change in the mug he kept on his dresser but only found another $3 and returned to the kitchen.

Sometimes there was money in the junk drawer. Kate tossed the old magnet that said *whoop-de-fucking-do*, a tiny birdhouse wind chime, and a little bud vase onto the counter next to the tomatoes and salsa, but she only found another fifty cents.

Kate thought about waking Ben. She needed help. This man wasn't going to just leave. Then she remembered there was cash in the emergency kit in the laundry room. She bumped her head on the door jamb as she climbed the stepladder. She cursed and covered her head with both hands. She was crying as she lifted the bin off the shelf, and when she dug through the granola bars and cans of beans, she found $20. She was still $1.50 short. $48.50. She reached for the knob and wiped the tears with the back of her hand while looking through a clear patch of glass. He was sitting on the bottom step— leaning back with his elbows resting on the next step. He was still there and she didn't have enough. She just didn't have it. Maybe he'd understand. Or, if it wasn't enough to get her the magazine, maybe he'd be happy enough to take the money and go away, to give up on this joke of a goal of his and leave her alone.

Kate had to shower and she had to have enough time to let her hair air dry. And she needed to find something festive to wear. Probably her green blouse but it needed to be ironed. Then she had to make her seven-layer dip and she had to make it just the way Julie liked it with the cheese and beans next to each other and extra olives on top. She had to make it the best she could, the best she'd ever made it. It had to be a work of art. It had to be perfect. She had to get rid of this guy because she had to make the best damn seven-layer dip ever. Julie deserved that much.

She walked to her purse and pulled out her wallet. She didn't know who to make the check out to so she left that line blank and wrote $50 next to the amount.

An hour later, Ben and Kate (with wet hair) got in the car to go to Julie's transition. As they drove, Kate went over her mental checklist: she'd given the man money, she was wearing teal (not black), and she had her dish. She hoped the man wouldn't come back and that Julie would have been pleased.

They parked across the street from the Center for Positive Living and were greeted at the entry by two young girls, neither of them Lauren, handing out origami tulips and programs with Julie's photo on the front. Inside, the pews were arranged in a half circle around a podium. Ben and Kate took a seat next to a fellow Tulip. Kate couldn't find Lauren. It wasn't until Kate was standing behind the podium with the rest of the Tulips, listening to the poem being read aloud, that she saw her. Lauren was sitting in the front row, in her favorite blue dress, her feet hanging off the edge of the bench. Kate smiled and broke apart her clasped hands to give her a tiny wave. Lauren smiled and waved back, just like it was an ordinary day.

Kate returned to her seat when the reading was over and folded her head down to her knees so no one would see her crying. Ben rubbed his hand along her spine. Kate heard the voice of the minister and when she lifted her head to blow her nose, Lauren was sitting on her dad's lap. Erik smoothed the back of her hair with his hand.

When the service was over, Kate caught Lauren's eye with a smile. They stared at each other while waiting to exit. Kate placed her open hands on her chest near her collarbone and said the word "I." Then she traced a heart in the air with her two index fingers and said "love." Then she pointed at Lauren. The last word, "you," came out like a yell.

The Oxygenated World

Their first fishing guide was a pilot who carried chocolates in his vest and plucked bugs from the air, smoothing their wings between his index finger and thumb while he matched them to his flies. Kate and Ben followed him through a New Zealand forest to a river pool so pristine it made Kate want to swim laps. He taught them to keep their arms between 10:00 and 2:00 as they stripped out line, forming soft loops in the sky. She was in love from the first time she placed her fly breathily on the surface. Catching the five-pound rainbow trout seemed gratuitous. It was almost too much.

As they hiked out, their guide told them about anadromous fish that were born in fresh water, spent most of their lives in salt water, and swam back upstream to breed and die. "Yes," Kate said. "They come home to die."

Back in Seattle, Kate became an amateur ichthyologist of sorts. In the years that led up to her diagnosis she read books about inland fish, freshwater and saltwater fish, and an entire book on the fish of Alabama. Her interest wasn't limited only to animals that swam; it included everything that happened under the water.

The chartreuse egg-sucking leech became Kate's favorite fly, not because she liked the way it attracted fish, but because she liked how the words rolled out of her mouth. She also liked to say anadromous, which sounded like Adriamycin, her first chemotherapy drug. She was comforting herself with this similarity when the doctor slid the door shut behind her and started talking about blood draws and infusions.

Kate leaned back into a vinyl recliner in the oncology ward and imagined the space as an ichthyology ward with aquariums full of fishes eating, breeding, and trying to swim upstream. The Ativan was working and she smiled sleepily at her husband Ben as her too-long bangs fell across her eyes. She couldn't see paying for a hair cut when it was all going to fall out in three weeks anyway. The doctor placed one hand on the back of Kate's chair. Even sitting, Kate was taller than the tiny woman, whom Ben called the pocket doctor, in her sensible shoes.

The doctor tilted her head, tucked her hair behind her ear, and asked how Kate was feeling. "Wondering if the chemo will work, right?" she said. "I'm sure it will be fine." Kate hadn't considered the possibility that chemo wouldn't be fine. "The nurse will watch you to make sure everything is okay. Any questions?"

Oh yes, Kate had questions. How had she ended up here in this bleach-scented room? Wasn't she just roll casting on the lake? Had she done something wrong? Had she angered Nereus, the old man of the sea and the Greek god of fish? She would never eat fish again. Purely catch and release. Forever. She promised.

That morning, after her first infusion, she opened her eyes with a start to see Ben staring at her. "Time for your shot," he said. He wasn't a doctor or a nurse; he was a color-blind software engineer who loved gummy bears and fish sautéed with garlic and butter. But a nurse had told him exactly what to do, and in the kitchen he filled a syringe from a practice vial of saline, flicking it with his finger to get the bubbles out. He punctured the skin of an orange. Kate didn't mind the sacrifice of fruit, they both preferred apples anyway. She liked hers sweet and he liked his tart.

Kate rubbed her palms on her thighs. Her short fingernails, the ends of hair brushing against her face, that itchy dry skin on her calves—it was all still there. The same. She worried the chemo wasn't working. She burped. That was new. That feeling stuck in the back of her throat, that tickle, the overproduction of saliva. She needed to throw up. She stood over the sink, looking into the drain, and reached for the bottle of anti-nausea pills while Ben pulled back the plunger of the syringe. She knew she shouldn't watch.

"Don't worry, Babe," he said, sticking the needle into the vial of medicine and pushing out the air before pulling the liquid into the canister. "I've watched Christopher shoot heroin on *The Sopranos* a bunch of times."

They went to the dining room table. Ben scooted his chair next to hers. She pinched the back of her arm, and when he wiped it with alcohol she could see his hand shake. The injection hurt like a razor blade cutting into soft skin. She told him to hurry. "Faster," she said. She rubbed her stung arm and twisted to watch the bruise form.

Ben kissed her cheek and locked the door on his way out, leaving Kate at the table amid the gutted *New York Times*. She rolled the rubber band from the paper between her index finger and thumb and tried to remember how to tie the fly line to the tippet. Was it the surgeon's knot or the clinch knot? She couldn't be sure. There was so much she didn't know.

While fishing was still fairly new to Kate, her attraction to deep water was not. She'd always been like a fluorocarbon line, strong and slender and quick to sink. In high school, when things went wrong, like when her government started dropping bombs or her friend Gary hung himself or she was in a car accident, she anxiously awaited swim practice. She would swim to the center of the pool over the spot where the shallow water descended to the deep and exhale, letting her body fall. She'd hide there in the world of oxygen deprivation, bouncing gently against the gunite bottom for as long as she could. When she resurfaced, she saw things a little differently.

Kate's doctor had given her permission to swim, and the pool air smelled clean like her high school hair, like safety itself. She slid $3.25 across the counter. The last time she'd been at a pool she was a lifeguard, lap swim was $1.25, and her mother still made her lunches.

When Kate jumped into the shallow end, she pulled her goggles over her eyes, raised her shoulders, inhaled, and sank into the cool water just like she used to. She stretched her body lean with her arms pointed over her head, clenched tight next to her ears, feet fluttering. After four quick laps, Kate exhaled, relieved to find that she still sank and that the pool was still quiet at the bottom. All she could hear was the faint rhythm of splashing hands and feet on water and she sat listening, suspended, waiting for something to happen. She hoped for some kind of inner healing, or conviction, or a sign that chemotherapy would work and that deep down, she knew she would live. She waited. Nothing. When her lungs could no longer take the pressure, she watched the swimming bodies for an opening; when the time was right, she kicked to the surface to re-enter the oxygenated world.

The following week, the pocket doctor leaned against the window in the exam room and crossed her legs at the ankles while she reviewed Kate's blood work.

Kate thought about surgeons and sturgeons. "The nausea is terrible," she said with a long slow exhalation. This was part of how she kept from barfing. "I don't think the meds are working. Carried a big bowl around the house all week."

"How about we try a different one?" the doctor suggested, crossing her arms around the file.

"And a liter of saline?" Kate asked.

"New med this week and saline next."

"How about both this week?" Kate gave the doctor her sweetest smile.

"I have some questions," Ben said, looking up from the laptop resting on his thighs. He was entering the new data from Kate's blood work into the spreadsheet. "A few questions. About the chances..."

"I don't," Kate cut him off with a hand in the air. "I can't hear them. Even if it's only a really small chance. I have to assume the chemo will work."

"I need to know," he said, "so when you get upset, I can say the right things. I'll only tell you good stuff. Maybe we can go to another room. We can talk there."

"Sure. Sure," the doctor said, sliding the door shut on her way out.

Their second fly-fishing guide had taken them to a river on the other side of the mountains in Washington and taught them to cross-body cast into dark corners and mend their lines in running water. He was a short man who wore camouflage pants and drank maté with a silver straw. As the rain came down, they sat in a picnic shelter eating PowerBars and corn chips while he told them about how the rivers had changed. Dams had been constructed. Salmon, sturgeon, and even the three-spined stickleback had to navigate a series of man-made steps built to encourage the fish upstream. The force of the water flowing through the ladder had to be just right—strong enough that the fish were motivated, but not so strong that they were thrown downstream or exhausted by the journey. Sometimes the dams were too long or the water ran too fast, and the fish had to be driven around the ladders in trucks.

"Don't the fish know something is different?" Kate asked.

"Maybe that the water has stopped rushing," he said, "but they keep swimming upstream, pushing the front wall of the tank like nothing is different while they bounce over potholes and through intersections."

She wondered if some of the fish got confused and went the wrong way.

By the third week of chemotherapy, Ben was able to give Kate injections while sipping coffee and listening to the morning news. Kate got used to passing her days on the couch reading fish books or watching the sportfishing channel while slurping Jell-O from Dixie cups and smoking pot from Sunshine.

One night when Ben came home, she asked him to make Tater Tots for dinner. Kate didn't eat processed foods before, but she needed to stop losing weight and her doctor encouraged her to eat whatever sounded good. And man did she have the munchies.

"With catsup *and* mustard," she said.

"You're a complicated woman," he said.

On days when she felt good (usually the days before her weekly infusions) she'd drive down to the Ballard Locks and sit on the bench across from the underwater window to watch the fish climb their ladders. Every now and then she'd see one swimming in the opposite direction.

Even as Kate's energy waned she continued to go to the pool. Her hair smelled of chlorine the day after her fourth chemo when it started to fall out. Clumps of straight brown strands collected in the creases of her hand when she squeezed out the water after her shower. She put her favorite brush and blow dryer in the back corner of the vanity, under the pipes of the sink drain, and cried. If her hair had to go, it would be then. She would shave her head that day, while she was crying, and do it all at once.

Kate found Ben watching baseball in the basement and told him it was time. His tears looked like hers—ruinous. Kate covered the kitchen floor with old towels and placed a dining room chair in the center. Ben shaved most of her hair with a few long strokes of an electric razor. It fell quickly, rolling in clumps down her white shirt, over the denim on her thighs, and piling up on the floor. It fell like muddy water, forming puddles at the bottom of a steep road. She was glad there wasn't a mirror around. She didn't want to watch it fall. She ran her hand over her prickly scalp and rubbed her fingers around the cowlick on her crown.

While Ben rinsed and changed the blade of the razor in the bathroom, Kate knelt on the floor, pulling her legs under her body, her butt in the air, the way she used to sleep when she was a kid with a stomachache. If her head was closer to the ground, she thought, the remaining hair would make less of a mess as it fell. She rolled a few shafts between her index finger and thumb. They felt solid, like a collection of endings. It would be a long time before she saw her hair again. With six months of chemo and her hair growing about an inch a month, it could be a year before she could go hatless, if she could ever go hatless. Maybe she would die bald. Maybe she would never remember how to tie the tippet to the fly line.

Ben emerged from the bathroom holding the razor like a microphone. She explained why she was lying on the floor. But Ben didn't want to kneel so she climbed back into her chair. She wanted her head shaved clean, slick, and glossy, but when Ben took off the guard for a closer shave, he nicked the side of her head and she bled. He put the one-eighth-inch guard back, but by then she had two bald spots, one above each ear. The strip down the center was one-eighth-inch long.

"Do you want to keep it?" Ben asked, nodding toward the pile of hair.

"No," she said. "Don't know what I would do with it and I don't want it sitting around waiting to be discovered on some innocent Sunday."

When Ben asked if she would shave his head, she said it was a sweet idea and all, supportive, but really it just made two bald freaks walking down the street instead of one. But he insisted, so she ran long slow strokes through his dense brown hair. It was an even one-eighth inch except for the back of his head where two cowlicks stood like rooster tails. While he cleaned the mess, she went to the bathroom and stared at the stranger in the mirror. Her skin was the gray color of her sweatshirt. The pink that used to be in her cheeks surrounded her eyes.

That night Kate covered her head with a blue bandanna so Ben wouldn't wake up to an ugly bald wife. In the morning, in the shower, Kate placed her hands flat on the back of her head and pulled them forward. Her palms were covered with dark stubble. She repeated the motion until her head was shiny and then she felt the lump in her breast, hoping it would feel smaller but instead, she was sure it felt bigger. It had gone from a quarter, flat and hard, to a golf ball, big, round, and spongy. She covered her bald head with a knit ski cap and got in her car. She didn't have an appointment so she waited in the lobby for two hours until a nurse led her back to an exam room. Kate held her shirt over her head and the pocket doctor poked around while Kate promised that she wouldn't just release, she would stop fishing completely. She would do whatever it took. She would only watch the fish climb their ladders. Only fish appreciation from there on out.

"Smaller," the doctor said. "Marble." But she still scheduled an MRI for the following Monday.

Their third fishing guide was a cattle rancher who spoke softly with a lisp. "Not all fish swim upstream to die," he said. "Sturgeon make the trip every year. They're smart, and when they're lost, they know to wait until the rain comes to wash the silt and minerals into the water, making fish pathways. They've ridden in the truck. They've seen your fly and they know what it takes to slip the hook."

Kate navigated the white hospital halls to the room with the MRI machine and positioned herself face down on the table. "Easy listening or rock?" the technician asked, placing earphones on Kate's head. She was careful not to bend her left arm where the IV entered her vein. And while the machine hammered, she wondered which was the proper term for a vegetarian who ate fish—piscatarians or piscavores—and if there was a word for people who ate all meat except fish. When it was time, she felt the contrast dye enter her vein, wet and cold but burning.

Kate's bare scalp didn't change the rhythm of her breathing or the grip of her stroke. That evening while she waited for her test results, she still pushed off the wall with her head down, her arms straight and tight behind her ears, and her toes pointed. She watched the small tiles in the center of the lane pass in front of her nose. From far away they looked navy blue, but up close she could see they were black with blue-gray specks and gray-blue grout. Kate counted each square. When her glide stopped, she pulled her hands in an arc around her head, like two question marks facing each other, bringing them down near her chest to a straight line ending at her thighs. She kicked, bending her knees, bringing her feet toward her body then pushing them out and together. She broke the surface and took a breath.

It wasn't long before she felt the familiar draw to the bottom and dove deep. She stopped. Exhaled. Sank. This had become her routine—to sit, suspended, underwater and wait for her conviction. As Kate looked up, she watched the air bubbles trying to escape through the mirrored surface and when she thought her lungs would burst from the pressure, she imagined her tumor in green, dissolving into bubbles that escaped through her skin as air. As she pushed off the bottom, she realized the nausea was gone and for a minute, she felt fine, just fine.

The doctor knew not to waste time and the next day when the results were ready, she came right out with it. "The tumor was reduced from the original 5.2 centimeters to 2.5 centimeters." A marble.

One night as the weather grew warmer and the chemotherapy treatments wore on, Kate and Ben decided to go fishing. Actually, Kate couldn't fish; she told Ben about her promise to Nereus. She would watch.

They were the only people at their favorite alpine lake that night. The only ones who knew the secret: The lake was warmer in June than August. But Kate didn't know why. Maybe it was because there were more daylight hours near the solstice. Maybe it was because the fall turnover actually happened in the summer. Maybe the northerly winds of August blew the warm top layer of water to the leeward shore forcing it down deep, pushing the cold water to the surface. There was so much she didn't know.

At first Ben and Kate swam. The water was still and reflected the moss-covered diving rock and the full height of the cedar and fir trees. When Ben dove off the rock, his kicked-back leg slapped the water.

As the sun slipped behind the trees, Kate swam over to Ben. She couldn't stand it any longer.

"What if tonight is my perfect cast," she said, her mouth hovering just above the surface. "What if I miss it?"

"Don't let it pass you by," he replied with a smile and a full backstroke.

Kate started to swim with long, gliding breast strokes away from the shore, but the bugs were hatching off the water, flying into her mouth.

"Maybe the wind will pick up and I can practice my double hall cast." She turned back to Ben.

"Opportunities like this don't come along every day," he replied.

A fish rose with a splash between them. She promised she would release. She promised.

Kate stepped into her waders and belly boat, attached her fins, and kicked to her favorite part of the lake, shady and filled with fallen trees. She started with a caddisfly. She wanted to use the chartreuse egg-sucking leech, but it was a wet fly and not right for the evening hatch. It only landed on the water twice before it was taken. She stripped in the line and tried to keep up the tension while letting the fish run. It was a brown trout and once in the net, it was still. Its scales were cool and soft to the touch and smelled like deep, clear lake water. She held it in her hand, admiring the delicate jaw as she pulled out the hook. She felt bad. It looked like it hurt, but she'd read that fish can't feel around their mouths. When the trout was free, she held it underwater, one hand forming a loose circle, the other stroking its belly, coaxing it to fill its gills.

Eventually it wriggled from Kate's hands, and as it swam away, an osprey dropped down to the water like a stunt pilot, before leveling out to glide a foot over the surface. It stopped, pulled the blades of its wings vertical, swung its talons forward, and snatched the fish from the water. The move was quick and decisive. She squinted to see water running off the fish and scales reflecting the dying sun. The bird brought its wings down with extra force, and as it gained elevation it turned the wriggling fish face-forward, streamlined to the wind. Nereus would be angry, she thought, as the bird and fish disappeared around a cluster of trees. Maybe she should have protected the trout, but when it swam out of her hands, it was no longer hers. The bird was hungry, the fish was food, and in the end it had nothing to do with Kate.

Sticky

Kate's dog is afraid of leaf blowers, and she used to think it was funny when the neighbor's gardeners arrived and he started digging into the ground or the fence or whatever he was near when the blowing started. When she found her lump, she began to understand the kind of fear that made that dog dig.

After Kate finished chemotherapy and her mental faculties began to return, she started looking for the cause. As far as she could tell, they had killed that damn tumor and she didn't want it coming back.

So, on a cold December night, Kate sat down at her computer to start reading through the 9.5 million links Google returned for "cancer causes," copying the ones that resonated into a small black book she kept in her pocket.

1. Water bottles. *Bisphenol A, which leaches into food from plastics and imitates hormones, has been linked to breast cancer and reproductive mutations.*

2. Water. *A study conducted by the National Institute of Environmental Health Sciences showed an increased number of bone tumors in male rats given water high in fluoride.*

3. Computers. *The National Cancer Institute (NCI) reported that children living in homes with electric and magnetic fields greater than .4 microtesla (usually found under power lines) may have an increased risk of acute lymphoblastic leukemia. Magnetic fields around household appliances, such as computers, can be higher than near power lines.*

An hour later, with only fifteen links down, Kate started to worry that, at this rate, the time it would take to process 9.5 million links (approx. 633,333 hours) would be detrimental to her health. She decided to ask the women at the cancer clubhouse because who would know more about what caused cancer than the women who had it?

Martha, who had the look of an honest woman, the type who put her real weight on her driver's license, leaned toward Kate and said, "I was healthy when I found the lump. No family history." She pulled a stainless steel water bottle from her purse. "Plastics were designed to disintegrate quickly in landfills and they break down in our water and food, entering the bloodstream and building up in our tissue."

Kate already had this one, but she wrote it in her book again, like she was casting another vote.

Patty, who wore solid blue pants and a matching blue top, was pregnant and working as a doctor when she found her lump. "Cows," she said. She hadn't had a drop of milk or a bite of red meat since diagnosis. Kate wrote it down.

Later, Martha told Kate that even when Patty was out of her scrubs, she wore one (and only one) color at a time. Kate could see where Patty was coming from. There was something pleasing about monochromatic simplicity in their complicated world.

A tea candle glowed from a table as Debra told the group about the dark night when she fell. "There was no moon," she ran her flat hand over her bald head, "and the street light was burned out, and I didn't see the ice and my foot slipped, and my ribs landed on something hard in my bag."

Kate ran her finger along the corner of her notebook.

Three years earlier, Debra's doctor had removed a 2.5 centimeter tumor from her right breast and pronounced her disease-free, but she still did four months of chemotherapy and six weeks of radiation to be sure. After her fall last month, the pain persisted, and she got an X-ray to see if bones were broken. They were not, but the film showed white tumors in her lungs.

"I stopped counting when I got to twenty," she said, picking at a handful of popcorn. "It looked like a blizzard." Then after a pause, "My oncologist said I'll probably die in the next year." She looked at each woman as if she was hoping someone would tell her it wasn't true.

Patty touched Debra's shoulder and said, "Two years ago my friend Margaret was told she had six months to live. She's still alive."

"I just read an article in *The Wall Street Journal*," Kate said. "They're close to a cure."

"Lance Armstrong," Martha said.

4. Cows. *In 1989 the FDA stated that growth hormones used to stimulate milk production in cows are absorbed by humans and thought to produce rapid cell division and multiplication that could promote breast cancer in adult females.*

5. Medical degrees. *Women who pursue advanced degrees are more likely to delay childbearing, while women who give birth in their early twenties are less likely to develop breast cancer.*

6. Pregnancy. *During pregnancy, high levels of estrogen cause cell proliferation promoting the growth of tumors, resulting in an increased breast cancer risk.*

7. Birth control pills. *The Collaborative Group on Hormonal Factors in Breast Cancer found that birth control pill users had an elevated*

risk of developing breast cancer. The risk was higher for women who started using the pill as teenagers.

8. Popcorn. *In a study published in the* Archives of Environmental Contamination and Technology, *rats fed genetically modified corn for ninety days showed signs of liver toxicity that could lead to cancer.*

9. Snow. *Particles of air pollution are absorbed into the water supply, becoming acid rain (or snow) which contributes to 550 premature deaths (some due to cancer) each year.*

The next meeting was cancelled because of the President's Day holiday. While Kate waited for March, she thought more and more about Debra. Maybe *thought* wasn't the right word. At first she obsessed. She couldn't sleep at all. She could only think about why Debra had cancer. Then, when Kate did finally sleep, Debra chased her through dreams.

Debra didn't come to the March meeting. They met in the same room but Kate sat in the wingback, Martha in the rocker, and Patty, in her green dress, on the end of the couch.

"My wig rubbed against my hair stubble," Patty said. Martha nodded. "It hurt. It turned my head all pink. So when the boys were asleep, Jeff would close our bedroom door and I would sit on the floor in front of the TV, leaning against the dresser, while he put long strips of duct tape on my head and ripped them off like a scalp waxing. I watched Letterman and bit my lip to keep from screaming and afterward I'd rub my flat palm over my head and say, 'Baby, you're the best.'"

"Now that I have hair again," Patty continued. "I've banned duct tape from the house. We use masking tape, or if we need something for plumbing, we use Mr. Sticky's Underwater Glue. Unlike some people," she looked at Martha, "I'm not afraid to be sticky."

Kate wrote *dressers, duct tape, glue.*

Every woman had her own phobias. Martha, who was diagnosed when her doctor biopsied some green nipple discharge, was afraid of things that stuck and spread—not just cancer, but cream cheese, bacteria, water drops on dry sponges, dandelions, bird wings, ants, bunnies, small pox, the bird flu, syphilis, duvet covers, blankets, beach towels, sprinklers, athletes foot, warts, search parties, spatulas, and ice.

When Kate's pen was still and the room quiet, Martha, who was almost a year out of treatment and disease-free (as far as she knew), told the women she saw her oncologist after she heard about Debra's recurrence and asked for a scan.

"He said, in his official doctor voice," Martha pushed a curl from her forehead, "'You know, statistically the chances of a scan catching an asymptomatic tumor are extremely low. It's not worth the extra radiation.' And I said: 'But it happened to Debra, and Debra isn't responding to chemotherapy. Her tumors are still growing and she's sick and she has a little boy who is only six.' And *he* said: 'She's not responding? It's a shame she knows. If she hadn't had the X-ray, at least she could have enjoyed the summer.'"

There it was. Martha leaned against an armrest, pushed her glasses up on her nose, and said her scan was clear and so did Patty. Kate had a clear scan last month at the end of chemo. She crossed her legs at the knees and again at the ankles like a cinnamon twist donut, and wrote "donuts." When it was time to leave, she closed her book, pulling the elastic strap around the outside and releasing it with a snap.

10. Dresses. *Perchloroethylene, or perc, is a clear liquid with a sharp odor used by most professional drycleaners because it removes stains from all types of fabric. It is also a toxic chemical shown to cause cancer in rats and mice when swallowed or inhaled.*

11. Dressers. *Particleboard contains formaldehyde. In 2004 the International Agency for Research on Cancer concluded formaldehyde was a "known human carcinogen" that caused nasal cancer in rats.*

12. Glue. *Contains formaldehyde (see #11).*

13. Duct tape. *Contains glue (see #12).*

14. Donuts. *Women in the top quarter of blood sugar readings have a twenty-six percent greater chance of developing cancer than those in the bottom quarter.*

As Kate sat down on the couch at the next meeting in April, she noticed the days were getting longer. Patty, in yellow, was running her fingers through her short ponytail and talking about selling her salad spinner at a garage sale last weekend.

"I washed my wig once a week in the sink and dried it in the salad spinner," she said. "Now whenever I see that spinner I feel nauseous and unsure if I am going to live or die. It's been sitting in the dark on the bottom shelf ever since."

"How do you dry lettuce?" Kate asked as she wrote, *salad spinner*.

"I use paper towels," Patty said. "Pat, pat, pat." She bounced her flat hand up and down on her thigh.

Debra, who was over her sinus infection, arrived late and sat cross-legged in the wingback, eating animal crackers from a box. "You know," she said. "A metastatic diagnosis isn't the end of the world. There are two things you have to do. Take a vacation every six months, and get out of bed every morning right when you wake up."

Debra squeezed the armrest and said she'd been feeling good lately—better than she had in months. She'd been enjoying the spring sunshine and planted a vegetable garden. Yesterday she noticed holes in her broccoli, picked three green caterpillars from the stalks, and with the toe of her shoe, squished them into the slate of her walkway.

"What would the Buddha do if a caterpillar was eating his broccoli?" Debra asked Patty, who was a Buddhist.

"You're growing broccoli?" Martha asked.

"I killed those caterpillars. Should I have moved them to my neighbor's garden? I mean, they were eating my broccoli."

"I like broccoli," Martha said.

"What makes you think it was *your* broccoli?" Patty said.

15. Salad Spinners. *Contain plastic (see #1).*

16. Sinus infections. *Women who take antibiotics for more than 500 days or have more than 25 antibiotic prescriptions over a period of 17 years are twice as likely to develop breast cancer.*

17. Sunshine. *Research shows the risk for melanoma, the most serious form of skin cancer responsible for an expected 8,110 deaths in 2007, is associated with the intensity of sunlight a person receives over a lifetime. The risk increases with increased time outdoors. The best prevention for melanoma is to shield skin from the sun with clothing and sunscreen.*

18. Darkness. *The NCI reports that vitamin D metabolites may help prevent cancer of the breast, colon, rectum, and prostate. The most reliable source of vitamin D is unfiltered sunlight.*

19. Sunscreens. *Even weak sunscreens block the body's ability to convert sunlight into vitamin D by ninety-five percent (see #18).*

Soon it was May, winter had turned to spring, and Kate still didn't really know Debra. She asked her to meet for a cup of tea and a walk around Green Lake. The deciduous trees were still naked against the gray sky, but Kate was looking forward to seeing their new leaves and being able to differentiate the robinia from the mimosa.

In the café Kate held her tea with both hands, letting the steam gather on the pores of her skin. "I look like Michael Jackson in the early years," Kate said. She used to have long straight hair. Now it was short and curly.

"You do not," Debra said, touching the curl above her right ear. "My ionic hairdryer works so well on frizz, it changed my life."

"I'm using this great new crème on my hair," Kate said. "It's spelled with two e's and no a's and that means it's extra good."

When it was time to walk, Kate stepped into the bathroom. She opened her book and wrote blow dryers and was looking at sunshine and thinking about applying some sunscreen. Then she decided maybe she shouldn't go outside at all. She was leaning against the wall with her notebook open when Debra came in to find out what was taking so long.

"Sometimes I just get stuck," Kate said. She pushed the bathroom door and then the café door open and stepped into the sunshine.

"Do you? Do you ever worry about what caused it?" Kate asked.

"What do you mean?" Debra said, lengthening her stride onto the trail. "Like genetics, pollution, that kind of stuff?"

Kate nodded.

"Nothing I can do about it so there's no use worrying, right?" Debra said.

As they merged onto the trail, Kate wondered if Debra would be dying if she had worried about it.

"How are you feeling?" Kate asked after a pause. "I mean, how are you feeling about what the doctors are saying? About the end-of-life stuff?"

"I'm worried. I won't lie," Debra said. "I'm afraid of death and the end, and what happens when it happens. I'm not a religious person. I just don't understand what kind of god would make my family suffer this way."

Kate jumped to the side of the path, startled by a man gliding past on roller blades.

"My husband and my son," Debra continued. "They're so alike. They're always at each other's throats. They drive each other crazy. What will happen when Alex is a teenager? I need to be here for them. If there is a god, he won't take me away. They need me." She turned to look at Kate, then touched her arm and pointed to a soaring bird.

"Eagle," she said.

But Kate could see five of them and she knew eagles didn't travel in flocks. "Vultures," she said. She thought of her Native American friend who said valleys and low points were created where soaring vulture wings hit the ground.

20. Ionic Hairdryers. *Household appliance (see #3).*

21. Hair Crème. *Parabens and phthalates are chemical preservatives that, when absorbed through the skin, act as estrogen in the body, disrupting normal hormone function and increasing the risk of breast cancer.*

22. God. *The spiritual laws God sets in motion, of obeying him and loving others, are self-enforcing, bringing down their own punishment in the form of suffering.*

23. Suffering. *Extended suffering stresses the body, increasing the pro-duction of hormones, and can lead to unhealthy behaviors (such as overeating, smoking, or abusing drugs or alcohol) that may affect cancer risk.*

24. Circling Turkey Vultures. *In the 1960s a gas company repair crew found a leak in their lines by watching for circling turkey vultures that were attracted to the scent of the gas. These birds didn't cause cancer, but they were attracted to the particles in the air that did (see #9).*

In late May, Debra emailed the group to say she wouldn't make the next meeting. She said her oncologist was out of drugs. He'd tried everything and the lumps in her lungs, and now her liver, were grow-ing. She asked if anyone knew anyone who was working with a new drug or a potential cure because she knew it was almost here and she just needed a little more time. At the end of the email she said, "Thanks for letting me be so naked and vulnerable with my request. It's one of the greatest treasures of this group."

Kate left her toxic computer and headed to the bathroom. It was her favorite room of the house—the communist dictator powder room—with a Castro bobble-head, a Mao clock, and a Stalin por-trait. She needed to feel the walls close and sat on the toilet. She stared at the razor in the shower, trying to think of reasons that she would be safe—she ate vegetables (so did Debra), she took her medi-cine (so did Debra), she exercised (so did Debra).

Kate sat in the bathroom for an hour because, although there was sunscreen, hair crème, and blow dryers in the particleboard cabinets, no one could force her to use them and she could stay there sheltered from cows, snow, computers, water bottles, dry cleaning chemicals, donuts, bird wings and vultures, salad spinners, antibiotics, and God. She looked at the image of Mao on the clock—and the counter-revolutionary waving the red book with the ticking seconds—and thought surely that God had overlooked this room. When she was finally ready to leave, the lock on the door stuck. She was trapped, but she jiggled the knob until it released.

25. Communism. *In the McCarthy era, water fluoridation was a suspected communist plot designed to poison Americans and destroy the United States (see #2).*
26. Razors and deodorant. *A study of 437 breast cancer survivors found that women who used antiperspirants and deodorant, and who started shaving their armpits before they turned sixteen, were diagnosed with breast cancer at a younger age than those who did not.*

At the June meeting, in the room with the high ceilings and the shades and the fake ficus growing in the corner, Martha asked Patty how Debra was doing.

"She's not doing well," Patty said, arms crossed over an orange T-shirt. "Sleeps mostly."

"Is she seeing anyone? Visitors?"

"She could have enjoyed the summer."

"Last week I brought her some nice blankets."

"Was she cold?"

27. Fake plants. *Real leaves and needles filter the air we breathe by absorbing carbon dioxide, carbon monoxide, sulfur dioxide, and ozone. Cancer-causing pollution from one car can be absorbed in*

a year by four hundred growing trees. A study conducted in Japan found that men who hiked in the forest every day had, on average, fifty percent more of the cells that destroy cancer cells than those who did not.

28. Cold. *According to traditional Chinese medicine cold can enter the body through a common cold or flu (see also #16), by not dressing adequately (see also #10), and by consuming cool foods and beverages (see also #1, 2, 4, 8, 14, 15), and if it stays, it can cause breast cancer.*

Debra died on the Fourth of July. While the fireworks exploded, Kate sat in her bathroom wondering if there was some significance to the date. Why the Fourth? Was Debra especially patriotic, a Republican or a Democrat? Was it twenty-nine days before her twenty-ninth birthday or six days after her son's sixth? If there was some meaning or symmetry, then perhaps it would be easier to understand why she died. Maybe then Kate could believe it "was her time" or it was okay, or that everything would be all right with the world again someday.

The next day the temperature reached ninety, and even the snapdragons and petunias lay down on the toxic dirt. Kate was supposed to go to support group but there was sweat, sweat everywhere. And no antiperspirant. Ben was at work, the dog was under the deck.

Maybe it was the heat or the hormones or that clock, that goddamn cheap wall clock, with plastic rim and dumb Roman numerals. When it hit the concrete patio, the glass broke but the frame stayed intact. The old stained oven mitt was next, ripped from the thumb to wrist, splitting white stuffing, sure to cause lung cancer, all over the kitchen floor.

Kate had been avoiding those dishes. They were such innocent little plates with their scalloped edges and small pink hand-painted roses. They were her great-aunt's plates—Aunt Punch, who died of ovarian cancer before her fortieth birthday. Before that they'd been her Great-great-aunt Mary's dishes. She died young of an unknown disease. Now the dishes were Kate's.

Kate lifted the first plate over her head and threw it onto the concrete without a care for her shins or the dog who was smart enough to hide when shards of porcelain began to fly. The first crash was the most rewarding. When the dinner plates were gone, she moved to the tiny dishes that were for salt or butter and flung them against the brick retaining wall like Frisbees. When the bowls were gone, she pushed the porcelain into a mound and used a hammer to break the remaining pieces until only powder remained.

One handful at a time she moved the pile to the corner of the yard, next to the lilac. She wanted to keep the powder; when the dog died she would put him there in the same spot. She wanted them to become part of the same soil, wanted the powder to feed her lilacs like lime.

The pile was complete when she heard the neighbor's leaf blower start. Kate sat cross-legged in the grass and called the dog to sit in her lap. She covered his shaking body with her arms and torso as the motor roared. The gate unlatched. Ben asked if she was okay.

"It's just so fucking hot all the time," she mumbled, head down, covering the dog.

"What's this?" he asked. She looked up as he found a pink rose still intact. "Are these your Aunt Punch's dishes?"

"We weren't safe," she said stroking the dog's head. "We weren't safe until they were all gone."

He shook his head. "I thought you liked them."

"I did," she said.

29. Fireworks. *The EPA states that fireworks displays release percholorate into bodies of water. Percholorate is a dangerous contaminant that interferes with the uptake of iodine, which is essential in the formation of thyroid hormone, and as a result, essential to overall health and immunity.*

30. Leaf blowers. *Chronic exposure to diesel fumes can cause inflammation and histopathologic changes in the lungs, and long-term exposure is likely to pose a lung cancer hazard.*

A month later, the group met on a misty evening in the heat of summer. The shades were open and it was still daylight. They all sat in chairs facing the foggy street. Kate thought of the inventor of the foghorn who heard his daughter playing the piano on a misty night and noticed the low notes traveled farther than the high.

"I'm not really afraid of dying, I'm afraid of a long slow death with my boys and husband watching."

"Her garden. She just planted her garden."

"It's supposed to be even hotter next week. I hope it gets enough water."

"Will someone cook the broccoli for Matt?"

Kate was afraid of dying by herself. She used to like being alone but that was before she started her list, when she wasn't afraid of fog and rain, wind shifts, cumulus clouds, high tides, dry sand that shifts under bare feet, bleach, moldy lemons in the fruit basket, slimy chard in the vegetable crisper, butter melting in the summer sun, chocolate sundaes, apple pie, and, really, all things American.

"The funeral was beautiful. All the different parts of her life were represented. She would have been pleased."

"She didn't even get to taste her broccoli."

31. Fog. *Above-ground nuclear weapons tests contribute airborne radioactive particles to the atmosphere that fall to the ground to be ingested and inhaled by people and animals.*

32. High Tide. *Studies have found that red tide (algal bloom) can cause respiratory problems including lung cancer.*

33. Dry Sand. *Radon, a radioactive gas released from the decay of uranium rocks in the soil, seeps through the ground and diffuses into the air. Radon gas exists outdoors and accumulates in areas without proper air circulation, substantially increasing the risk of lung cancer.*

34. Wind shifts and cumulus clouds. *Increasing incidents of lung disease can be partly attributed to breathing in tiny particles of sulfur and other pollutants from power plants.*

When they met in September, the shades were up and a radioactive breeze flowed through a window near the fireplace. Fake ficus leaves rustled. A new girl, Linda, wore a blue bandanna. She had almost finished chemotherapy. "I think I'm almost ready for reconstruction," she said. "My dad offered to pay because he says that no one should have to buy their own breasts. The surgeon's going to move a muscle from my back to my chest. That's the first surgery, then I'll have three adjustments." She reached behind her head and tightened the ends of her bandanna. "It's like getting a suit tailored, you know; you've got to go back for alterations to get it just right."

"I finally picked up my new prosthetics," Martha said. "And they feel huge even though they're smaller than I used to be. They feel like watermelons."

The word "watermelons" drifted up to the ceiling in the breeze and through the fake ficus leaves until there was a bang on the closed window like the slap of a flat hand against glass. Kate looked down to the radon-laden concrete and saw something. She ran downstairs.

A tiny bird was lying on its chest, stuck to the ground, tilted slightly to the left with its neck and needle-thin beak extended and wings spread over the dust. Its brown head and tail were the shade of her dog's fur, and she could barely see the iridescent crimson of its neck glittering like a band of sequins. Kate knelt on the sidewalk, pressing her palms into the concrete to get a closer look at the bird. Martha knelt beside her and a tear dropped from her chin to the dusty pavement.

"I wonder why she wanted to get inside," Martha said.

Kate wanted to write down *windows*, but just then, Patty leaned out the window, and Kate knew the hummingbird had been aiming for Patty's red T-shirt and capris. Maybe it was hungry and thought Patty was a hibiscus, or maybe it was attracted to the simplicity of a monochromatic world. Kate thought of writing *red*, but realized that she would also have to write *yellow* and *orange*, and even if she'd written every color, this bird still would not have been safe.

Kate leaned back, holding her left hand to her chest with her right. The bird's heart pounded like a dog panting, and Kate was not sure if it would get up. It could just be a matter of time. A few minutes. A horn honked. She looked at the dahlias that lined the sidewalk and hoped the bird would get to enjoy one more taste of flower. Kate wanted to reach down and slide her palm under its chest, to touch its head and tell it everything would be all right, to carry it to a nearby dahlia. But she stopped herself because she knew that if this bird was going to make it, it would have to get up on its own.

Made of Metal and Constructed with Fire

My welding instructor, Bean, is an artist and regular welding savant. He carries photos of his favorite work—the Statue of Liberty reclining with a cocktail entitled *Lady Liberty Takes a Break*—in the front pocket of his Carhartt overalls. At our first class, he's wearing safety glasses with stars and stripes running along the temples. He gives me a handout and says it's written in iambic pentameter. When I say, "Really?" he says, "No, but wouldn't that be cool?"

We meet on the south side of Seattle in a cinderblock building that used to be a Wonder Bread factory but is now filled with sanders and saws. I sit on the rickety stool, place a bag with my glasses, leather gloves, and pink cap near my feet, and start reading the safety handout. Soon I'm wondering if my prosthetic breasts are flammable or if the metal particles in the air will increase the chances of growing tumors in my lungs.

Bean starts class with introductions. Yes, he says, his birth name is Bean—it isn't a nickname. I like it, not just because it's one letter off my husband's name, but because he says his parents named him after that funny British TV show. When he's done, we continue introductions around the table—a lawyer, an illustrator, an architect, an engineer, and me, the woman writer. I'm here because now that my treatment is over, I've decided I need to make something. We have a beach house with a narrow bathroom and custom cabinets that need to be replaced. I've decided to make tables, but not out of any perishable wood silliness. My tables will be made of metal and constructed with fire.

Bean spends the next four hours telling us how every machine and tool in the shop can kill, cut, maim, amputate, burn, or crush. The band saw, the Beverly shear, power shear, belt sander, disk sander, chop saw. These are gloves to keep you from sanding off your knuckles. This is a shower to put yourself out if you are burning. This is the guard, make sure it's down. Wear the face screen. Cover your eyes. Sand your splatter.

He pushes through the double doors to the outside work area. "If this thing," he says, scooting an anvil set on a block of wood to the center of the group, "like, fell over, it would crush your ankle like a potato chip. Has anyone ever been to a 7-11 in Japan? It's a junk food mecca—best junk food in the world. You know, this is a nice anvil. It has a nice ring to it." Bean hits his hammer on the metal. "Hear that? Probably a $1,400 anvil. Use your shoulder to hammer, not your elbow. We're going to heat metal up and bend it. This is so easy. I can make a fairy wand." He lifts a piece of metal, twisted at the top, and waves it in the air. "See? Wheee! Pay attention now. Don't blow yourself up."

I look longingly at the tanks and torches lining the wall and as I follow him through the double doors back to the classroom, I realize the first class is almost over and I haven't made or burned a thing.

"I'm tired of explaining things to people," he mutters. "I need a vacation in the country."

I'd just returned from my own little vacation in the country—the forest really. It was a breast cancer retreat where Ben and I spent the weekend talking about our feelings, practicing yoga, and eating homegrown vegetables. Joe, our facilitator, had a neatly trimmed beard and at our first group session he slouched in his chair with his legs spread wide. He wore boots that looked normal from the front but when he turned his feet I noticed there were heels, like women's shoes, but the stem was a spring and a flat rubber sole met the ground. He spoke slowly in a soft, almost feminine voice and told us he'd just returned from the Sound Healing Conference. He had survived prostate cancer and saw his illness as a gift that helped him identify the priorities in his life. "I'd like everyone to sigh with me," he said, letting out a groan, arms hanging to the floor. "Just let it all out. Come on, everyone with me now."

Ben sat to my right with the bill of his red baseball cap pulled low so he didn't have to look at Joe. He fiddled with the welt on the arm of the rumpled couch we shared. I could tell he was wondering how he ended up here.

One of my support-group friends had recommended this retreat, saying she hoped it would help me find peace and clarity. My treatment was over but ever since Breast Cancer Awareness Month, I'd been obsessed with survival statistics and terrifying "news" stories. I wouldn't have minded a little peace, but I mostly wanted a weekend in the woods with my husband.

When I'd mentioned the retreat to Ben over dinner, I smiled and raised my eyebrows. All he said was, "Am I going to have to talk about my feelings? Because I prefer to keep that stuff hidden deep inside." We both knew he was joking and we both knew it was true.

"Probably," I said, "but I hear the food is good and the rooms are nice."

He rolled his eyes in resignation and I signed up the next day.

Joe reached under his chair for a wooden bowl. "It's not perfect," he said. "It has holes, knots, chips. I want everyone to take a minute to put their judgments, worries, and criticisms into the bowl for the weekend. You can have them back on Sunday night."

After the bowl had made its rounds, Joe brought out a talking stick. It was broken and fragile, covered in lichen, wrapped at the base in green ribbon. The retreat would have been a whole lot better if that stick talked but, to my disappointment, all Joe meant was that the person who held the stick got to speak.

"Tell your story," Joe said. "And think about this: what do you want to be in your heart when you die?"

Kristina started. The bangs of her wig hung down into her eyes and her cheeks were swollen from the steroids. "The first doctor asked me how my marriage was and told me to find Jesus. He didn't even examine me. A month later, the cramping got worse and I made an appointment with another doctor. The next day he took a grapefruit-sized tumor out of my abdomen. It had already spread to the brain. I used to think I was indestructible but now I know anything can happen." When she was finished, I exhaled louder than I intended.

At the next welding class, Bean is through with safety. He starts by showing us where to find the oxygen and acetylene tanks, how to open the valves and adjust the gauges, how to attach the tips to the wands and get sparks from strikers. When I ask, he promises I'll get to melt metal before the evening is over.

"I hope you all enjoyed National-Talk-Like-A-Pirate Day yesterday," Bean says, setting up his welding station.

I sit on a stool and cross my arms to keep myself from reaching for the torch.

Bean walks to the stereo. "Opera is for melting metal," he yells over the roar of an aria and a band saw. "Later we'll have sitar for sawing and banjo for bending."

In the crescendo, I recognize the aria from *La Bohème*; it's my favorite. It's right after Mimi "drops" her key in Rodolfo's dark apartment and their hands touch accidentally, when they're falling in love. It's before Mimi gets sick, and before Rodolfo blames himself for her cough, for his drafty bedroom, and for not keeping Mimi safe.

When Bean returns to his station, he lights his torch with the sound of a match hitting water. He tells us to cover our eyeballs and adjusts the yellow flame until the blue cone at its center is a quarter-inch long. "Be sure to cover," he says. "Your skin won't just blister, it will peel off in sheets." He adjusts the oxygen and holds the wand in his leather-covered right hand. "Concentrate your heat on the base metal," he yells, bringing the flame down at a right angle and forming a red puddle. "Hold it. Here. In the same place until you punch through. I want you guys to practice this."

When he punches through, he yells, "Welding will make you free!" Even with my dark goggles, the spark is brilliant. The metal pours over the edge of the table like a bucket of water but light and spindly, thin and bright, and each drop bounces along the concrete floor like the ray of a sparkler.

"Pretty soon," he says, stopping his flame with a turn of the knob, "you'll be able to make porcupines and sell them at craft shops in Cannon Beach."

When the demo is over, I go to the spot where the metal bounced across the floor and pocket a hardened droplet.

I chose that particular weekend to go to the breast cancer retreat for a reason.

"Seemed like an okay way to spend the day," I said later that first night when we'd returned to our environmentally friendly room with cork floors and counters made of cashew-shell resin. "Do you remember what today is?" I asked, looking for the toothbrush in my toiletries bag.

Ben stared at me in the bathroom mirror, flossing his front teeth. His expression did not change. He rested his floss-wrapped fingers on the counter. "Hmmm...no birthdays, not Mother's Day..." Finally he lifted his hands. "Yes, it was the day we took the stuff and did the stuff." He moved his bound index fingers in opposite circles. "You know, and then we were really happy." He looked at me with a big smile and raised eyebrows.

"I've been talking about this for weeks," I said. "Are you kidding me? Do you *ever* listen to what I say?"

He said he really couldn't remember, and when I reminded him it was my first cancerversary (the anniversary of the day I was diagnosed), he said, "Oh, sorry, Babe, that's a day I try to forget."

The next morning, even though Joe didn't have the stick, he said, "Death is a rumor, something you hear about and know must be true, but is always off there in the distance, happening to someone else. You think you're safe until it comes to you."

Sarah had the stick and said she felt bad she was in the room with us because she had a tiny tumor and no chemotherapy or radiation. She had the "easy" kind of breast cancer.

It came to me next and I rolled the stick between the fingers and the thumb of my right hand. "I was diagnosed with inflammatory breast cancer, stage IIIB, eighteen months ago, at the age of thirty-one. I had twenty-seven weekly chemotherapy treatments, a bi-lateral mastectomy, and radiation. Now I am cancer-free but the odds are not good. Ten percent chance for five years." I paused and twirled a ringlet behind my left ear. I didn't cry. I twisted the twig with one hand and the curl with the other. I looked at the ceiling and thought about what a terrible job someone had done mudding and taping the sheet rock. Actually, the mudding and taping were fine, they just hadn't sanded, and I wondered why they hadn't finished the job.

"One of the things that bothers me most," I said, "I mean, since the surgery, is that now my heart is exposed. I don't miss the breasts. Well, of course, I'd rather have them than not, but I haven't considered implants because, really, I'm totally over breasts. But now there's nothing protecting my heart. When I shower I watch it beat—my skin pulses. When I cross my arms, I feel it, and I know it could stop at any time."

Joe slouched farther. "We can put a face on our demons," he said. "It's okay to see them for what they are. To invite them in for tea."

I handed the stick to Ben, who wiped a tear from the corner of his eye. "I guess I hadn't spent much time thinking about the possibilities. That this might come back. What might happen." I patted his hand to encourage him. It was about time.

"We should think of our bodies as gardens," Joe said. "To nourish physically, emotionally, and spiritually. We need to heal all the aspects of ourselves."

Oh, yes, I thought. *I'd like to heal spiritually.*

Even though I didn't have the stick, I raised my hand and asked how to do that.

"Well, how do you heal spiritually?" Joe repeated. "You're asking how to do it? Um. Well. You could... That's different for everyone. For some it may be discovering what you believe. For some, reconnecting with a religion; for others, letting go of control. Everyone needs to find their own path. Have you considered a vision quest?"

I nodded. I thought of a movie I'd seen years ago, *Vision Quest*, about a high-school wrestler in love with an older woman. I was pretty sure Joe wasn't recommending I take up wrestling, but I had an equally hard time picturing myself on the other kind of vision quest—alone in a forest, smoking peyote, and examining the contents of my soul.

"You create your own beliefs," he said. "After all, they're just thoughts elevated to truth."

We're well into our second class by the time Bean finishes his demo and turns on some bluegrass. I know what that means—time to bend, not burn. He shows the class a small metal box he's been carrying, tucked under his arm. Then he makes his way around the room, talking to each student. When he gets to my station, I show him my homework, a match-box template made from a file folder. While we're talking, I pull out the drawings I've made for my tables. I have the measurements from the house and have already decided the legs will be one-inch-square bars and the tops will be sheets of metal bent to form trays. I've signed up for the tile class and even chosen the small brown glass mosaic tiles to cover the surface.

"Have you thought about a career in welding?" he asks, inspecting my drawings.

I blush, looking down. "How could I? I've never welded before."

"Your time will come," he says as he turns toward my neighbor.

I'm still carrying the metal pellet I found after the demo, and as I reach into my pocket, I picture myself with my pink welding hat turned backward and my face shield pulled down, holding a torch over a bent sheet, constructing perfect joints.

Bean shows us where to get the sheet metal and how to measure and draw out the proper dimensions on it. Then he shows us how to bend the metal and fill the seams. Now I know everything I need to complete my project.

He leans over the barrel of scrap metal and says, "Try to use as many scraps as you can because, after all, nothing leaves this planet unless it's a satellite."

He tosses a piece of metal into the bin. "If you do a good job tonight," he says, "in the next class, I'll teach you to weld with a car battery and a coat hanger."

Cheryl had the talking stick next and told us about her stem-cell transplant, watching her blood filter through the tubes. "All my white blood cells were destroyed," she said, "and for days I had no immune system. I was completely exposed and now I feel like I can't count on anything."

By then I'd had enough of Joe's gift and wanted to break that damn stick. I had to get out of the room. As I was planning my escape, Joe decided to take everyone outside for a rainy walk through the labyrinth made of lavender. We were instructed to wander the maze searching for our individual paths.

While Ben and I waited for our turn, we sat on a bench under a cedar tree and talked about our departure the next afternoon. Would we take the ferry or drive back to Seattle? When we were the only people left, we stood, and as we walked, I whispered that we should take the ferry and stop to look at art galleries on the way home.

"You know I don't like to shop," he said, twisting to see me around his hood.

"This isn't really shopping; you like art." My feet crunched over gravel.

"You should get home to rest."

"No, I'm fine. Please. Come on," I said to the back of his coat.

"Maybe I'll barbeque some steaks for dinner," he said.

We'd arrived at the center of the circle but I was unsure how we got there. All I knew was that when we were newlyweds, he would have gone shopping. And when I was in chemotherapy, we always did what I wanted.

"I just want to be normal," I said. "To drink mochas and wander around."

"We haven't had any meat all weekend," he grumbled, turning toward the exit. "Your hematocrit is probably down again. You're going to overdo it."

I reached for his arm to make him stop. "I just want to be young and in love again." A stream of water ran off the side of my hood. He didn't notice my tears among the drops of rain.

"We can be young and in love while we rent a movie and eat steak," he said, his shoulders hunched over his arms that stuck straight down into his pockets. He stepped over a lavender hedge on his way to the dining hall.

As the second class nears its end, I know melting metal is inevitable. I listen carefully every time Bean walks to the stereo, knowing I will burn stuff soon.

I wheel an oxy-acetylene tank to the far end of a metal table. I put on my safety glasses and uncoil the hoses. I clean and attach the tip. I open the tanks and check the gauges. I place the wand in the holder clamped to the table and arrange my bricks next to each other, sheet metal resting on top, welding rod to my right. Magnets nearby just in case. I sit on my stool, wobbling back and forth, and double-check my supplies. I take off my glove and set the pellet from my pocket on the table. I've got everything I need, and I'm just waiting for the opera to begin.

Ben and I didn't speak as we ate our organic, vegetarian, gluten-free lunches. Our continued silence suited the yoga studio, where our teacher instructed us to stand back-to-back, our heels touching. When I stood straight, my bottom fit into the space at the top of his thighs. His bottom fit into the curve of my lower back. My shoulders fit against the incline of his middle back. We pushed our chests out. The back of my head fit into the curve of his neck, just below where his skull rose and covered my head. Our hands touched palm to palm as we lifted our arms straight from our sides. We reached toward the ceiling and as our arms extended, my fingers slid across his palms, resting at the bases of his hands where they stopped when we reached our full extension. Then our arms slid back down to our sides. With our newfound balance we leaned into each other, fitting together in all the right places, and reached for the ceiling a second time.

After yoga and dinner, as we prepared for bed, I pulled off a piece of dental floss. Ben spat toothpaste into the sink and picked up the floss container. "Did you get this out of the garbage can at home?" he asked.

"Oh, yeah," I said, moving the floss through my teeth. "I couldn't imagine why someone would throw away a perfectly good container of floss."

"I dropped it in the toilet." He emphasized the last word.

I carefully unwrapped the floss from my fingers.

"Do you always go through the garbage?" he asked. "Can't you just trust the floss was there for a reason? That I'm looking out for you?"

"I've been using this toilet floss," I said, laughing a little bit, "for like two days."

"Someday you'll thank me for this," he said. "You'll thank me for protecting you from the evils of contaminated floss."

Then the music starts and it's *La Bohème* again, but we're no longer at the beginning. We're already in Act IV, when Mimi reunites with her lover to die. She and Rodolfo are reliving their early days together. Bean tells us to light our torches. I check the gauges a second time, and as Rodolfo's tenor crescendos, I straighten my pink hat and slide on my leather gloves. I clench the striker and pull my hand back when the flame erupts from the tip and sputters into the air. Even with my ear plugs in, the sound of fuel and fire is loud like an auditorium of applause. The flame is neat and narrow and licks upward at the end. I twist one knob and bring the flame down to a pointed thread. As Mimi and Rodolfo talk, the strings are sweeping and melodic and it seems as if everything will be just fine when the oboe comes in and is joined by a single clarinet. It's all sweetness and love until the coughing starts and Mimi loses consciousness.

The blue diamond at the center of the flame intensifies. "Float your torches down onto the metal," Bean yells, striding among the tables to check each student. When Mimi's friends join them in the apartment, they whisper, like they don't want to wake her. They're just waiting for her to die. It's time. I reach across my chest and feel my heart beat. For a moment I imagine my next welding project, a suit of armor molded to my chest exactly, but I quickly refocus when Bean moves past my station. I push the torch closer, perpendicular to the metal. When the wind instruments start with all their pomp and brass, it's clear she's dead. The words don't matter. It's the tragic pulsing of the horns that delivers the news. The strings come in as the weeping starts and the pounding of a snare drum announces the full depth of Rodolfo's grief. The music is loud enough to be heard over the burning, and as I move my torch closer the sheet turns red and blisters. As the flame punches through, Rodolfo runs to Mimi's side and cries out her name.

I can no longer hear Bean over the sound of the full orchestra. I still believe in his instruction, but there is no room for anything other than music and fire. And suddenly, as Rodolfo calls Mimi's name for what I know will be the last time, I feel clean and free of poisons, gifts, and even statistics. My healing has begun. I don't care about patterns, holes, or lines, the end product or the art, the metal matchbox, or the tables. I only want the pleasure of watching drops of metal bounce across the floor as my sheet transforms from solid to liquid back to solid again.

Reconstruction

Ben and I go to Vegas hoping to bring home a baby. Susan, the birthmother of a six-and-a-half-pound African American baby girl, has chosen us, but she's a carrier of the sickle cell gene, and we want the baby's test results before we'll agree to the adoption. We've been waiting two days, when Dee, the agency social worker, says, *Look, are you going to adopt this baby or what?* and we decide to fly down from Seattle to try to make the adoption work.

When we get to our hotel room, I heave my suitcase onto the gilded couch, walk to the window, and throw back the brocade drapes. On one side of the Strip is a bare lot. It looks like a child's sandbox filled with bulldozers and backhoes. "I think that was the Stardust," I say, tapping my finger on the glass. "I guess they blew the place up so they could build something better."

Across the street from the sandbox that used to be the Stardust, the New Frontier Casino's sign looms over an empty parking lot surrounded by a cyclone fence. A backhoe raises its claw and picks at the wall of a small building, foreshadowing destruction. "I guess the same thing is happening here," I say.

Ben looks out the window. "If I saw someone pushing a stroller through a casino," he says, "I'd be thinking *What kind of a mo-ron brings a baby to Vegas?*"

The phone rings. When Ben answers, I can tell it's Dee by the way he pivots on his heel toward the desk, like he has something to write down, but then runs his hand through his hair. I push the small pad and pen toward him, just in case.

"Not until tomorrow," Ben says, snapping his phone shut. That's when Dee said the results would be ready. We'd heard this before. Our pediatrician says the test is required by the state but the baby's doctor says it isn't. Dee made a special request and the results are due any day.

"We should go to a baby store tomorrow," I say, opening my suitcase and placing a pile of hand-me-down baby blankets on the coffee table. I've wanted to go shopping since the first birthmother reviewed our profile six months ago. Her only request was that the adoptive parents not practice any formal religion. *A Heathen*, I thought. *Just like us.* That birthmother was Norwegian, which I knew would have made my dead grandmother so happy. We'd waited two weeks before Dee told us the baby had gone to another family. I suspected that the birthmother had known the truth. Maybe she'd recognized my short curls as chemo hair. Or maybe she could see the fear in my eyes.

"I want to be ready." I sit on the couch and scratch the sore spot on my ribcage with my right hand, like a monkey. My oncologist wants to know about any pain that lasts longer than a week. This is day three. "We can always return the stuff if things don't, you know, work out. We'll keep the receipts."

Ben wipes his glasses with his shirttail. "Diapers, wipes, formula," he says. "What else?"

"Bottles, onesies, burp cloths..." Ben's cell phone rings. He raises his hand to stop me.

I picture a tiny baby cupped in his palm.

After a fried food dinner, Ben falls asleep while I watch the evening news. An orange-skinned man says the sixty-five-year-old cowboy-themed New Frontier Casino, famous for its bikini bull-riding contest and the home of Elvis' first Vegas show, is slated for demolition in two days. But the demolition company still has to place 1,000 pounds of explosives in 6,200 locations, and it appears to be running behind. The crew is working around the clock.

I reach up and close the drapes. The New Frontier parking lot looks like a ball field lit up for a night game, and I think of sweet five-year-old Cheryl. We weren't set on adopting a newborn; we were willing to consider any child up to the age of six. Cheryl had straight blonde hair cut at her jaw line, blue eyes, and small gray teeth. She loved baseball. She'd been taken from her father's home where she was sexually abused by her seven-year-old cousin. Cheryl wore a turquoise peasant skirt and tennis shoes to the afternoon game that stretched into evening. I slathered sunscreen all over her neck and shoulders, and when she finished, Cheryl said, "Feels like you've done this before." When her foster mom came to get her that night, Cheryl didn't want to leave. But we were just babysitters. Cheryl did leave and six months later she went home to live with her dad.

Before I slip into bed, I unclasp my silver chain-link bracelet woven with red thread. Ben and I bought it at a market in southern China after a bald Chinese woman told us that every baby was connected to the important people of its life by an invisible red string tied around the ankle. I fall asleep wondering if this baby's red string is weaving its way toward us right now.

The next morning at the baby store, a tall slim woman with dark skin and prominent cheekbones asks if we need help. I wonder if Susan's bone structure is angular or soft and if her eyelashes are long or short.

We make a pile next to the register, and while I decide whether to buy the organic cotton swaddle blankets for $5 more, Ben investigates diaper bags, settling on one that claims to have a "system." He likes systems. When we've collected all the necessities—fingernail clippers, the pacifiers like the hospitals use, bottles, formula—I go to the toy aisle and find a cream-colored duck made of organic cotton. Its body is a round rattle the perfect size for small baby hands. I put it on top of the pile because I want the first thing we buy for the baby to be something she can really hold onto.

When we step up to the register, the cashier's large firm breasts loom under her sheer turquoise shirt. *Surely they aren't real*, I think, but neither are mine. After my bilateral mastectomy, I purchased stick-on prosthetics. At first, I wore them stuck to my skin every day with my old underwire bras. Then spring came, the sun came out, and I started sweating. I come from a long line of big-pored people, and when I sweat my skin gets itchy and irritated. I cleaned them every night, carefully scrubbing each one with a special brush in a circular motion for three minutes. One day I realized I was spending forty-two minutes a week—almost three hours a month and thirty-six hours a year—scrubbing breasts. That day, I covered their sticky sides with felt and had pockets sewn into my bras.

The cashier is bagging our purchase, and Ben is swiping his card when I lean toward him and ask, "Do you want me to have breasts?"

He glances at me before entering his PIN. "Huh?"

Maybe I should have breasts if I am going to be a mother. We've been waiting so long I'm starting to think the maternal god of children wants me to be whole again before giving me a baby.

"I mean do you want me to have surgery?" I ask.

The clasps on Ben's sandals rattle with each step through the parking lot. I know he knows what I'm talking about. A few weeks ago, Ben was in the room when the bow-tie-wearing plastic surgeon ran his fingers along my scars, looking for lumps. While he worked, I stared at the skin stretched tight over the waves of my ribcage, the reddish-purple radiation outline, the tattoos the technicians used to align the machine. I still didn't consider this chest to be mine—I'd always had perky C-cups that held their shape without a bra.

When the plastic surgeon finished tracing my scars, he moved to my abdomen. With a pinky at each hip bone and thumbs at my bellybutton, he squeezed. Then he reached for a small ruler and measured my fat roll and moved the ruler from my abdomen to my chest. Eventually he said that after nine hours in surgery and two days in intensive care, he could probably get one breast out of my abdominal fat but that "it might look a little funny, like an orange sliced in half." The other breast would be an implant inserted between my muscle and my ribcage.

"Well, if you can't feel anything, it doesn't seem worth it," Ben says finally, pulling out of the parking lot. The doctor said I'd never have sensation in my chest again.

"You're still talking about me," I say looking at the side of his face. "Do *you* want me to have breasts?"

"Well, I guess," he says and shrugs.

"I read this article," I say, while we're stopped at an intersection. "It said breast cancer is five percent more likely to occur in the left breast than the right, and the left side is known in Chinese medicine as the maternal, nurturing side. Maybe I need to get in touch with my nurturing side." The light changed and I wondered if maybe just getting one breast done would be enough.

"I don't want to see any more doctors," Ben says.

On our way back to the hotel, we drive by the New Frontier. The biggest building, the hotel, is missing one column and three rows of mirrored windows. Some of the empty frames are covered in black mesh while burgundy drapes billow from others. The "E" from Frontier spelled vertically down the side is gone. It's already a different hotel. Now it's the Frontir.

Ben sits on the gilded couch in our hotel room while he leaves a message for Dee. I fold and refold the piles of blankets and burp cloths. It's day four and the pain in my side reminds me of Sara. She and her husband had completed their home study and were waiting to adopt when Sara had a recurrence. It was in her bones but the growth was stopped by a hormone-blocking drug. She and her husband still wanted a baby but they couldn't find a social worker or agency who would work with them. They even went to court, but the judge said they couldn't put a child in the home of a dying woman.

Ben's phone rings and he sits on the edge of the bed. I sit next to him, trying to connect with his brown eyes, wishing he would tip the phone away from his ear so I could listen. Instead I flick the clasp on my bracelet.

"Tomorrow," he says when the call is over. My shoulders drop. I've heard this too many times. "But she says we can go to the hospital tomorrow." He raises his eyebrows. "Susan is signing the relinquishment papers tonight and even if they don't have the test results tomorrow, we can talk to her doctor." The baby was in intensive care receiving a week of preventative antibiotics after an unplanned home birth.

I gasp and clap my hands together. This is good news. I shiver a little in the cold draft of the air conditioner. Because we are in Nevada (unlike California, Texas, or Washington), Susan is allowed to read their whole home study, including their health histories. Like Christopher's mother, Susan could still change her mind.

Christopher was a cute kid, without any major behavioral problems, other than a little lying and occasional stealing (which Dee assured her was common for children of neglect). He said he wanted a family with three dogs, a cat, and "cows that roamed freely." Christopher's father raped his mother in front of him when he was two and his father's rights had been terminated. Christopher's mother suffered from post-traumatic stress disorder and agoraphobia and she said she would relinquish her rights, but in the end she couldn't sign the papers.

Over lunch, when Ben asks where the baby will sleep, I cover my mouth.

"We have to go back to the baby store," I say, my mouth full of fish taco.

When we get to the aisle with the playpens, I tell him we need a green one. "Why not blue?" he says, scooting a box to the side. "Since we don't need a noisemaker."

"Yes we do," I say. "We need the noisemaker. It's soothing. And we need a mobile. A mobile in primary colors because that's all babies can see, and I want it to move on a timer." I push past him and lift the giant box into the cart. "And we'll need the changing table and the one with the different height bassinette because when she's older we'll want the bottom lower so she can't climb out. Do you want her to climb out?" I'm moving toward the checkout when I feel the pain in my side. It's a sharp poke, like a reminder, but it's still day four and I'm pissed because I don't need to be told twice.

The woman with the large breasts is still working, and as I pay, I decide that if this baby doesn't work out, I'll get new breasts. Maybe like this woman's or maybe just a bit smaller. We push through the automatic doors into the afternoon shadows. Next to the street, there's a woman with long red hair flowing down her back. She's waiting at the bus stop with a huge roll-away suitcase. She's eating some kind of meat stick or sausage from a can, and when she starts drinking the liquid, I stop. She looks just like I'd imagined Cassandra to look.

A few months ago, we reviewed her profile. Cassandra was nineteen years old and admitted to drinking every day of her pregnancy. I knew we'd have to turn this mother down, but I'd continued to read. Cassandra was a homeless, recovering meth addict who'd served time for assault and battery with a deadly weapon after a fight with her boyfriend. She loved to sing and was a cheerleader in high school. She had a child when she was sixteen that was born with "a disappearing brain" and died before its second birthday. Cassandra's only hobby was writing poetry.

I look back at Ben who is trying to make room for the playpen in the already full trunk. There's so much stuff. I wonder how we will get it home. I consider shipping it or maybe buying another suitcase. The bus arrives and I watch the woman haul her giant bag on board, one step at a time.

Back at the hotel, I set up the playpen while Ben orders an evening snack from room service. We watch a movie and Ben falls asleep. I lie awake worrying about how we will clean bottles without a kitchen and blankets without a washer.

I drag an armchair to the window. There's activity all around the New Frontir on its last night—bulldozers, backhoes. I count seven waiting street sweepers. There's a crowd of people gathering behind the fences. The orange moon rises fast and clean, reflecting off the hotel's toothless grin.

I think of the boy with the disability we'd heard about only a week before. Dee called on a Friday night and told me in a breathless, rushed voice about the five-day-old baby with the deformed hand. Dee needed to know, right away, if we wanted to adopt him.

Ben and I researched and talked for an hour. Ben didn't want to deal with more doctors or surgeries. But we'd been waiting so long. And who was I to reject someone based on a physical imperfection? After an hour, I called Dee and told her we couldn't adopt the baby.

"May I ask why?" Dee asked.

"Well, it's the hand," I said.

"*You* haven't even *seen* it," Dee said.

I cried then and I cry now as I wonder if we were supposed to adopt that baby.

Ben gets out of bed and pulls up a chair as the countdown to demolition starts. Giant white sparklers run a line from the entrance of the parking lot to the casino, like the burning wick on a stick of dynamite. When the trail hits the hotel, fireworks explode from the roof—blue and green. The number ten lights up on the side of the building, then nine and eight. When the countdown reaches zero, the image of a handle appears and descends onto a box of dynamite until dust and smoke explode from the three floors that were cleared of their windows. Those floors collapse. I know the big boom is coming, but I'm startled when the surge shakes our building. I feel it in my chest. Then the collapse starts on the left side of the hotel and moves to the right like dominos falling until all that's left is a plume of smoke and debris stretching into the sky.

We listen to the machinery start up. Gradually the cloud of golden dust, illuminated by the glow of their building and the full moon, settles over the wreckage.

"Do you think anyone will miss it?" I ask without moving my eyes.

"Maybe some of the locals," Ben says, "who lived with it and knew it best."

I feel the pain in my side and realize I don't have to tell anyone about it if I don't want to.

I wake Ben at 8:00 a.m. so we can go to the hospital. When we're parked, he opens the trunk to grab the diaper system. I pull the duck from the end pocket and tell him we don't need the rest. "We'll just see how it goes," I say.

Ben tosses the bag back in the trunk.

"Isn't it a cute duck?" I admire its yellow beak and decide to keep it, even if the baby doesn't work out. "We should give it a name."

"How about Chicken?" Ben says, walking through the sliding doors. "Hate to tell you, Babe, but that's no duck."

We walk past the front desk, like we know what we're doing, and stop in front of a hospital directory. My eyes move to the oncology ward, but I force my gaze back up the list to the neonatal intensive care unit.

There's a baby dinosaur painted on the wall next to the elevator. Ben pats its head while we wait. A black woman walks past and I clutch the duck tighter. The woman is short and stocky with glistening straight hair. I wonder if Susan's lips are full or slim and if her hair is curly or straight. I hadn't considered hair. When Ben reaches over and rubs the head of the duck, I'm thinking about oils and braids and barrettes.

"You see that orange thing there?" Ben says. "I don't know what that's called, but I know ducks don't have them."

"So it's a chicken," I say. "Doesn't mean it shouldn't have a name."

We step onto the second floor and follow a pathway covered with baby dinosaur footprints to the neonatal intensive care unit where the six-pound, six-ounce, nineteen-inch baby girl is waiting.

We stop at the double doors. I peek through one rectangular window while Ben looks through the other. It's a sterile environment. We have to be buzzed into the locked scrub room. Beyond the empty nurses' station, there are four bassinettes made of clear plastic, each on a wooden chest of drawers, each with one end slightly elevated and a pink or blue blanket draped over a side.

I feel the sweat gathering on my scarred chest and the pounding of my heart on my nurturing side. I cross my arms around my middle and for the first time I touch the sore spot on my ribcage. I poke it. When I move my fingers, the lump moves too, like a knotted muscle. As I dig in deeper, the pain ricochets up to my shoulder. It's day five but I can think of a few hours this morning when I didn't feel that pain and decide it's time to start the clock over because I know there will always be some pain somewhere.

I look down, past my hands, to my feet. The edge of the dinosaur pathway is marked with a thin red line that runs under Ben's foot on one side and mine on the other into the intensive care unit. I stick my index and middle finger through the center of the ring-shaped chicken. I reach for Ben with my other hand. There's no one to let us in, so we wait. I can feel the oncology ward behind me, but I continue to look ahead, through the room and out the window. I can't see the casino's wreckage from here, but I know the lot won't stay empty for long.

While I'm staring out the window, a tiny hand catches my eye, fingers outstretched, reaching above the far right bassinette. I hear footsteps that sound like hard clogs hitting a hard floor, and a nurse rounds the corner, pulling off her rubber gloves and dropping them in the garbage. She gives us a small nod to tell us she'll be with us in a minute and turns toward the bassinette with the outstretched hand.

"Here she comes," Ben says without turning his head. "Are you ready?"

Epilogue

Today, August 4, 2011, I am over six years past my diagnosis and cancer-free (as far as I know). My recovery from treatment has not been easy. I've struggled with anemia, hypothyroidism, and endometriosis, but my progress has been steady.

A very talented and thoughtful team of doctors and practitioners works hard to keep the Katherine 2011 up and running. It's no easy task. I am what my sister calls self-sustaining high maintenance. I take a handful of vitamins twice a day; I adhere to a special diet devoid of gluten and soy. I drink tea, distilled water, almond milk, and sake (exclusively but never together). The person I used to be would roll her eyes at the person I have become.

Our beautiful daughter is approaching four. She is a fully charged powerhouse of a girl who wants to be a scary monster when she grows up. She loves twirling and dancing in tulle and sequins. She was born ready for any adventure. My husband and I have taken her sailing, skiing, swimming, canoeing and snow shoeing—she always wants *more, more, faster, Mommy, faster!* We're perfect for each other.

Just six weeks ago, we took custody of a deliciously sweet one-year-old boy. He loves to motor around the house with his little Frankenstein walk and pull on his sister's braids. He's easygoing and playful and his addition has brought our family into a perfect balance. We are, right now, exactly as we should be.

Many of my cancer-friends have gone on to do amazing things— babies have been born and adopted, specialized post-treatment medical clinics have been started, our local support group has tripled in size. One of these women, Judy Almazan Stuhmer, a talented graphic designer, created this cover.

Of course, some of us did not make it—Dena, Emily, Kelly, Kristin, and Elizabeth. These women were brave enough and strong enough. They wanted to live badly enough. They did everything right, but in the end, it wasn't enough. It doesn't always matter how hard we "fight" or how much chemo we can endure. Sometimes we do not control our own destinies.

Ladies, the world isn't as beautiful without you in it. You are missed.

Acknowledgments

There are so many people to thank for supporting me through my dark days of treatment and through the creation of this book.

First, my husband whose support in sickness and in health has never wavered.

Pam Houston who gave me something to look forward to when life was grim. She offered me a process of creation that enabled me to write in a new way, depth, and direction for each piece of work, and validation as an artist. Without Pam's generosity and wisdom this material would not have become *Who in This Room*.

Pam's writing program, the Pamfas. I learned so much from these women, not just from their critiques and workshops but from their lovely writing and approach to the craft—Karen Nelson, Susan Von Konsky, Peggy Sarjeant, Barb Matousek, Kae Penner-Howell, Karen Laborde, Lesley Dahl, Heather Malcolm, Tami Anderson, Cindy Newberry Martin, Sarah Phipps, and Christina Sbarro. I look forward to reading your works in print some day.

My Seattle writing group. They've continued to give thoughtful advice and direction even in the face of endless repetition. Patricia Smith, Joy Mills Parker, Jon Phillips, Peggy Sarjeant, Marilyn Dahl, Karen Franklin, and Sharon Reitman, thank you.

My agent, Elizabeth Wales of Wales Literary Agency, who supported the book well past the point it made sense.

Margarita Donnelly, Beverly McFarland, Kelsey Connell, and Rebecca Olson at CALYX Books for doing such important work and being so lovely and utterly reasonable. Thanks for making all of this possible.

The *Bellevue Literary Review* for awarding "Made of Metal and Constructed with Fire" the 2009 Goldenberg Prize for Fiction and publishing this piece in the Volume 9, Number 1 issue.

CALYX, A Journal of Art and Literature by Women, for publishing "The Oxygenated World" in the Summer 2011, Volume 26, Number 3 issue.

My family. My grandmothers who were both the perfect models of grace, style, and adventurousness. My parents who taught me the meaning of dedication and commitment. My sister, my partner-in-crime and tolerant recipient of random messages about reality TV and 80s pop stars.

The women of the Seattle-area Young Breast Cancer Survivor Support Group. I learned so much from you. You transformed my experience.

The friends who've brought soup, thrown parties, made Tater Tots, and been all kinds of awesome. How did I get so lucky?

Thanks to Judy Almazan Stuhmer for the book cover design. I couldn't love it more.

About the Author

Katherine Malmo is a Seattle-based mother, wife, and writer who was diagnosed with inflammatory breast cancer in 2005. These days she is cancer-free and blogs about adoption, race, health, and living a low-toxin life at www.hystericalmommynetwork.com.

Her work has received the 2009 Goldberg Award for Fiction from the *Bellevue Literary Review* and the 2007 Pacific Northwest Writers Association Literary Contest's award for Adult Short Story. Excerpts of this book and other stories have appeared in several literary and commercial publications, including the *Bellevue Literary Review* and *Gastronomica*.

Colophon

Titles in this text are set in Neutraface No. 2 Condensed.
Text is set in Garamond Premier Pro.